# TOWARDS A
# HUMANE ARCHITECTURE

# towards a
# humane architecture

## BRUCE ALLSOPP

FREDERICK MULLER

First published in Great Britain 1974
by Frederick Muller Limited, London NW2

Copyright © 1974 Bruce Allsopp

ISBN: 0 584 10301 8

*Printed in Great Britain by Bell and Bain Ltd., Glasgow and
Bound by Hunter & Foulis Ltd., Edinburgh*

# Contents

# Illustrations

# chapter 1
# The Present Dilemma

Man is, by nature, a creature of the surface of the earth. By the exercise of great ingenuity he has made machines in which to fly and has even traversed space, but in the astronaut's journey he goes from surface to surface; the anxiety is eased when he touches down. Above the surface man is out of his natural element and fears to fall or, even worse, to lose control and be projected for ever into space. Down below, men burrow into the earth but the subterranean world is dark and mysterious; the miner is recognised as having a tough and dangerous job. We are creatures of the surface living by the light of the sun. We stand upon our feet and for rest we lie down upon the earth. In ages before sophisticated knowledge obscured fundamental awarenesses man thought of Earth as a mother and as a goddess, knew that he came from the earth and returned to it remaining always a part of it; believed also that just as Earth was a goddess so he himself was likewise in some sense a spirit.

Modern civilisation has loosened our contact with the earth, made us less aware of our dependence, which is still entire, and inflated our pride which can be seen as a corruption of the spirit, for pride has no substance: it is a spiritual condition. But the earth is still under our feet and it is upon the earth that we build architecture. Truly fundamental to our architecture is the floor of our building, that upon which we stand, our point of contact. We first feel architecture with our feet.

About this we are very sensitive for the surface can vary from a filthy quagmire to bright polished marble, from water meadows to blistering sand, from silken carpets to encaustic tiles, from mountain tracks to oily motorways, from ice-floes to fields of wheat. We have need to be careful where we tread and our other senses, our eyes, ears, even our noses, assist in guiding our feet. We recognise the nature of a surface before we let our feet touch it, and as we now mostly wear shoes or ride on wheels our other senses have largely taken over from the sense of touch in our feet. Our eyes perceive but they do not directly feel, yet, because we

1

recognise what a surface will or would feel like under our feet, we
have built up a relatedness of feeling. Through eyes, memory and
association we know what it would feel like to tread on a jellyfish
or a hot iron foundry floor. We are also affected by other associa-
tions so that we recoil from a surface slippery with blood or
covered with the feathers of plucked chickens. Furthermore, we
learn to associate the appearance and feel of a surface with characteristic conditions and activities; the clinical smoothness and
hardness of an operating theatre which can be associatively rather
frightening; the luxury of deep pile carpets and silk draperies; the
earthy comfort of old oak and soft lighting in a bar parlour. Design
a bar parlour in the clinical manner and it will fail; but with a
hospital ward there is a dilemma which we resolve by choosing
hygienic efficiency, though patients might be happier, and so might
do better, in a more "homey" atmosphere.

The hospital environmental dilemma will be discussed later but
is mentioned at this stage because it presents, in terms of familiar
experience and obvious reasoning towards a generally accepted
judgement, the fact that the qualities of surfaces profoundly affect
human responses. The first surface is the floor and not only does
its actual surface matter but also our awareness of its relationship
to the earth below. To be in a hospital bed on the tenth floor is to
feel that much removed from the surface of the earth. People may
vary in their sensitivity to this removal, even to the extent of
throwing themselves out of a window—an event which I have
witnessed—and some delight in flying or climbing high mountains,
but they don't want to *live* up in the air. To the architect the whole
building rests upon the earth. He sees the building as a whole.
The occupant of an apartment is aware of the level at which he
lives as a lower boundary from which he descends to the ground
level from which he is aware of being removed. It is significant
that, ideally, old people's homes are conceived to be bungalows
with direct access to a garden—cottage homes.

We are concerned with horizontal surfaces, both as to their
nature and their position in relation to the earth. The floor is the
fundamental component in architecture. The floor is limited and
defined by vertical surfaces which may be quite low, as in an
Elizabethan garden, or which may rise to considerable height, as
in a piazza, but with the sky still open. Some of the greatest architecture does not enclose space but it does define it. The next stage
is complete enclosure and instead of the sky above we have a
ceiling which may vary from the rough undersides of beams and
boards to a great dome. Generally, architecture is an alternation

of enclosed and unenclosed space, the enclosed buildings defining the unceiled spaces and giving rise to the fallacious distinction between inside and outside architecture. One is as much in an architectural environment in the Piazza di San Marco at Venice as one is when one has passed through the portal into the Basilica. Architecture begins with the floor, the point of man's contact with the earth to which he belongs. It extends upwards and sometimes over, but the first touch-point is the floor—and then the walls which we can also feel, and appraise with a view to feeling, by means of our eyes. The ceiling is different and almost always differently treated. It is more for our eyes and ears, for the ceiling closes us in and sets a limit to vision in the direction of the sky and infinity, and it also affects the acoustics of the room which are so important for our apprehension and feeling for the space enclosed. The bright, hard surfaces of the clinic or the electronic control room give an acoustic quality matching the visual quality. The blind man is well aware of the different feel of a swimming bath, a cathedral, an operating theatre, a boudoir, a bathroom or a padded cell.

Our sense of smell is less frequently involved in our awareness of architecture; it is relevant in a church, a library of old books, a railway station or a public lavatory, but the other four senses are constantly involved in our awareness of architectural environment. With the growth of pollution, especially atmospheric pollution, the *absence of smell* becomes a quality to be enjoyed and, of course, in a garden there are situations and arrangements which can best be appreciated in the dark when scent takes over, and the moths awaken.

Architecture is not for architects; it is for people, and whatever architects may think and whatever theories they may have, it is through the senses that people appreciate, that people *feel* architecture.[1] One does not satisfy feeling by expressing one's own feelings, any more than one makes a wedding cake by eating the icing-sugar oneself. What is required of the architect is a mainly intellectual process based upon *sympathy*.[2] He must contrive to give to people what *they* will enjoy, not what he would wish them to enjoy because it is what he wants to do.

Probably all people who have a cultivated skill, whether it be in architecture, surgery, computer-programming, football, acting or embroidery, develop standards of judgement, criticism and conversation peculiar to their group. Thus a surgeon can perform an excellent operation, though the patient dies, and an architect can design a students' hostel which is the cynosure of professional admiration but creates detestable living conditions. This state of inward-looking professionalism is rife in all the arts and professions, perhaps as an escape from "the hog of multitude"[3] but it is a dead end. It is a major reason why modern architecture has lost the respect of common people. It has achieved Le Corbusier's objective of being for an élite, "for the chosen few",[4] but unfortunately it is a self-chosen few and, as might be expected, the standards have fallen, and to the common man it presents façades of icy indifference and often accommodation of prison-like austerity.

What has been lost is the artist-audience relationship and in architecture the audience cannot be selected; it is humanity in all its diversity and vulgarity. It is all very well for the sophisticated architect to recoil from the word *vulgarity* and be unwilling to recognise that in many kinds of building his design must have the common touch, but the alternative is everywhere to be seen, in modern architecture which in fact pleases nobody. Neither is the argument that economic conditions and attitudes make the satisfactory practice of architecture impossible a valid one for these very conditions have been aided and abetted by architects, underpinned by functionalism and depreciated by the creeping disease of cheapness. The cheapest way of satisfying the minimum standards of accommodation is no way to architecture.

People want architecture which is warm and comforting to the senses, architecture which is pleasant to live with, which caters for man as he is and not for man as an abstraction, architecture which is seen to be appropriate to its purpose, bearing in mind the habitual attitudes and responses of people who have been brought up in a living society, not processed in a laboratory. The supreme fallacy of modern architectural thought is that if the architect designs what he knows, by his own introverted standards of pure architecture, to be best, the public *ought* to grow to like it. Why the hell should they? There are people who delight in solving high-brow crossword puzzles but it is manifestly unreasonable to expect everybody to embrace this exotic form of enjoyment; likewise it is absurd to argue that in all things, including architecture, the public should learn to admire and enjoy what the experts say they should. The corollary of this would be that the experts should all suppress their own tastes, in matters other than their speciality, and bow down before other experts. Quite clearly this is not the case and I am reminded of the famous modern painter who told me he just couldn't stand this modern music.

Modern architecture has not only lost the confidence of the

public; architects themselves have lost the way. Even ten years ago there was a lingering faith in "the modern movement". There were great men, "pioneers of the modern movement" still alive, but who are their heirs? Who are the great architects of today? The modern movement has been exploited and debased by men whose principal qualifications are ability in handling committees and a gift for making money. Enormous world-wide practices, based on a kind of architectural baby-farming, *seem* to give opportunities to the young graduates of our schools of architecture who are sucked into these administrative machines for churning out buildings. The pioneers were dedicated to ideals and they did not become rich men. They were not necessarily always right but they believed in their modern movement. They may well have made a major contribution to the history of architecture but those days are over. Obviously a "modern movement" could not last for ever. It was a revolution and it happened between the first and second world wars. Every movement in the history of civilisation, and the arts of civilisation, has had a limited run—even the Renaissance—and the modern movement was not like that, though people involved in it tended to think it was at the time.

The modern movement is finished and what have we now? There have been gains and losses, the nature of which must be discussed in the following chapters, but in spite of our present disillusion I think the gains outweigh the losses. The modern movement was necessary. The prolongation of eclectic architecture, based entirely upon craft building techniques, was not possible. What we have had, in the modern movement of the 'twenties and 'thirties, was a puritanical revolution, a clearing away of a great deal of overgrowth, a simplification, a catharsis based largely upon a functionalist creed and a materialistic outlook. We are rapidly learning that unbridled materialism is destroying the material advantages it seeks to promote, that the pursuit of economic gain can diminish the standard of living, that functionalism as generally practised excludes many human values which matter more to people than the values it propagates, and that a true functionalism, properly taking into account all values and needs, would be so wide as to have no specific validity. The ideas and values underlying the modern movement are in question, as the result of experience and in the light of new thought. Economic, social and functionalist ideas of the 'thirties now seem pathetically naïve. Where do we go from here?

# chapter 2
# False Foundations

Modern architecture is a recognisable commodity all over the world and one is reminded of Le Corbusier's famous book, *Vers une Architecture*, towards *an* architecture, *one* architecture. It is to a large extent his child but like most offspring, not entirely what he expected nor what he would have approved. The most common complaint about modern architecture is the monotony, the fact that from Melbourne to Minnesota and Hamburg to Johannesburg, from London to Istanbul and Tokyo to Toronto, architecture is superficially the same—it is recognisably modern, and it seems that out of the stern principles of the pioneers, who rejected the idea of a style, and, like their Renaissance predecessors, based architecture upon universally applicable principles, a modern style has, nonetheless, emerged.

This is a repetition of what happened after the Renaissance when a system of design based upon classical principles led to a style of design which was practised by architects who knew little or nothing about those underlying principles. Thus, in the eighteenth century the architecture of Paris and Edinburgh, Bath, Nancy, Leningrad and Madrid was obviously of the same kind and the subtle differences meant little to the ordinary man, though to the modern historian of architecture these differences are important and easily recognisable.

If we look back to the beginning of the twentieth century, when the modern movement was emerging, nineteenth-century eclecticism was going out of fashion and the new schools of architecture, as well as the older ones in France upon which they were modelled, were restoring classical design. Blomfield in England and McKim, Mead and White in America are typical of this phase during which the Rome scholarship became a passport to success. It was against this revived-neo-classicism, this new architecture of humanism, that the modern movement revolted. Apologists and historians of the modern movement have traced its roots back to Victorian Britain, to the Arts and Crafts movement, to Morris and Norman Shaw, to Louis Sullivan in America, to Art Nouveau with its

6

The Municipal Building, New York City, 1908
Architects; McKim, Mead & White
(From *A Monograph of the Work of McKim, Mead & White*)

emphasis upon the exploration of new forms. According to the doctrine of the movement Gropius and his colleagues at the Bauhaus rescued modern design from its obsession with hand craftsmanship and related it to modern technology.[1] The shapes of things were to be the logical result of solving functional problems by the use of machine tools in accordance with the "morphology of materials".[2] Form was to follow function. Ruskin's lamp of truth was turned into a searchlight; all decoration was to be rejected and beauty was to be found in the functional shapes and inherent qualities of materials truthfully expressed. The history of medieval and vernacular architecture was bent in order to prove that architecture was the result of solving functional problems by the logical use of structural forms in accordance with the nature of materials and in relation to the climatic conditions.[3]

But the pure doctrine of functionalism made design into an intellectual process which modern artists instinctively rejected. Modern architecture naturally looked to modern movements in the other arts and especially to abstract painting. Le Corbusier made a synthesis in his own life-work, becoming much more famous as an architect but remaining, all his life, an abstract painter.

To some extent the forms which followed function and the forms which interested the abstract artist *seemed* to be similar. It was a misleading coincidence. Architecture is, by its very nature of serving the need of man for built accommodation, a practical, functional art; but by overstressing the functional aspects, to the exclusion of nearly all the activities which architects have always enjoyed, and apparently reducing architecture to an intellectual, problem-solving occupation, the functionalists encouraged architects to find opportunities for abstract design in architecture. But the leadership in abstract art lay with painters and sculptors who owed no allegiance to functionalism. *They* were concerned with form for its own sake and the nearest they came to functionalism was exploring for the forms which were appropriate to the materials they were using. (This idea certainly goes back as far as Michelangelo.)[4] So the paradox arose that the artistic and, as the architect understood it, the "design" aspect of his work, the component which really interested him as a creative artist, derived from painting and was *not* function-based. Thus the generality of architects developed a vague aesthetic in which solution of the functional problem, and truth in the expression of structure and materials, were the matrix from which he started to work as an artist and, in line with the psychological thinking of the time, to *express himself*, the converse of expression being inhibition. The supreme exemplar of this extraordinary compromise was Le Corbusier. He had the advantage of being a good abstract painter himself. In *Vers une Architecture* he had extolled the beauty of machines and coined the arresting phrase "a house is a machine for living in". But he had also been captured by the "pure form" of classical art, especially the Parthenon, and being a man with faith in his own originality, he looked at the social aspects of architecture, particularly housing, and created new ideas. He tended to express his thoughts in epigrams which give a specious simplicity to enormous problems—*La Ville Radieuse, L'Unité d'Habitation*, for example. Not only architecture but urbanism became a vehicle for abstract design into which man came, not as a reality, but as a symbol. The creation of subtle and beautiful relationships of form and space gained in precedence as he grew older and more masterly in his art, and his interpretation of function extended into the subliminal and the symbolic. The result was an architecture which achieved, without figurative allusion or traditional mouldings, some of the qualities of classical design, marred only by the poverty of the materials which he was constrained to use.

Allowing for a difference in scale, it could be said that Le Corbusier stands to the modern movement as Michelangelo did to the Renaissance. Ordinary artists cannot operate on such a level. Allowing for a difference of scale, Le Corbusier can be compared with Michelangelo who inherited the High Renaissance and foreshadowed the Baroque. Corb, as he came to be known to a generation of students, showed the way back from functionalism to art. He, more than anyone else, stood for the synthesis of function, social consciousness, structure, pure form and self expression. But art, for Corb, was abstract and he had his roots in the abstractist school of modern painting within which he was a reputable but by no means supreme performer. Abstract art, like functionalism in architecture, gives special emphasis to an element which is present in all art. It has been a fascinating excursion which cannot go on for ever.

Abstract art produces works which are entire within their own terms of reference.[5] It does not refer outside itself. When an abstract artist introduces a recognisable reference, such as the sail of a boat which suggests that the shapes refer to a river scene, his work ceases to be abstract and becomes "specific". By *specific* art I mean all art which refers to something which can be identified outside the work of art.[6] It may be an emotion such as grief, the words of an *aria* in an opera, the shape of something recognisable, an allusion, an analogy, a representation as in a portrait, a decorative form based upon nature, or even a recognised pattern, such as a *gavotte* in music. Nearly all art in the history of mankind has been specific but there has been an abstract element in it. The modern movement literally abstracted this element and made it the whole of art. By intensive study of this element artistic experience has been greatly enriched. Without such concentration much of the achievement of Paul Klee, Joan Miro, Ben Nicholson or Mondrian[7] would have been impossible. But we are now at the point where art must return to the mainstream, if only because it cannot forever concentrate upon its own *inner relevance* to the exclusion of its rôle as a necessary part of the means by which man interprets himself to himself.

*While artists have been withdrawn into their own abstract world hosts of new problems have arisen which require artistic interpretation, and in the sociological context it is fair to speak of the "treason of the artists" because of their escapism into a tiny world of abstraction when humanity was confronted with the greatest challenges in all its history.*

In this book we only look backwards when we must, and agreement or disagreement with the propositions I have just stated must depend upon reading about the history of modern art in the many books which are available, but I would ask the reader to remember that the history of modern art has been written by people who were far from dispassionate. Every movement which succeeds gathers a host of outriders, like the lackies of a seventeenth-century prince, who identify themselves with, and derive their income from, being in the "outfit". There will have to be a reassessment of the history of modern art in the light of what comes next. It would be naïve to pretend that art history is not susceptible to the influence of what has succeeded and it deals harshly with lost causes. I do not think abstract art will prove to have been a lost cause but it is a dead end, and in the reaction which is on the way it may suffer undeservedly. Sociologically this suffering may be necessary because it is essential that art should come back to *life*.

The great majority of architects do not originate: they imitate and adapt. Imitation of the essential qualities of a genius like Le Corbusier is impossible but the idea of treating buildings as compositions in abstract form can be applied by anybody with varying degrees of success. Many schools of architecture now begin their courses with the study of "basic art"[8] in order to develop the design abilities of the student so that he can use architectural programmes as a medium for abstract art.[9] Some people, including Le Corbusier himself, have tried to formulate theories of abstract design but most people seem to trust to intuition and this gives them the opportunity to believe that the designs they create, though abstract, are also personal and thus a means of self-expression. It is thought to be important to express oneself and many people think that this is what art is about.[10]

But architecture is not an abstract art; it is highly specific and, in Philibert de l'Orme's phrase, concerns the *"comfort and convenience of the inhabitants"*.[11] Furthermore, functionalism, one of the foundations of the modern movement, is not concerned with art at all: it is concerned with the efficient solution of problems in practical ways. What results may be thought beautiful but it is no more a work of art than the Grand Canyon, unless you distort the word art out of its normal meaning.[12] So it is not surprising that many architects and thinkers about architecture have rejected art altogether and chosen to regard architecture as a non-artistic, practical, problem-solving, constructive activity. In between, there are those who believe that insofar as one achieves a beautiful artifact this process is indeed true art. Hence it may be argued that by the study of building science the creation, by means of scientific and technological devices, of a satisfactory environment *is* the art of architecture. It may be admitted that intuition, the use of a cultivated human brain, is preferable, at any rate in our present state of knowledge, to the use of a computer, but the artistic activity is really seen as a way of resolving competing claims which is analogous to, but more efficient than the computer for the time being.

So within the "modern movement" in its terminal stage of transition into something else, we may have a strong anti-art component which stands upon the original foundation of functionalism and may well be called neo-functionalism. It is entirely reasonable, within its own terms of reference but, like so much scientific and technological thinking, it closes its eyes to what it does not understand, by pretending that art is not there, when, in fact, we know, from the whole of human history, that it is a very real and necessary part of life. And the real proof of the pudding is in the eating: architecture as an abstract art may have become trite and boring, because abstract art has run its course, but the buildings which are designed by functionalists are far worse. They look like filing cabinets for human ciphers. Mere functionalism does not work.[13]

It is an understandable reaction to retreat from the incomprehensible and bewildering into a sensible and rational situation and this is happening in the architectural profession throughout the world in varying degrees but perhaps most of all in Britain, a country which is going through a phase of being terrified of thinking fundamentally and philosophically. The social rôle of the architect is being stressed. He is a member of "the building team". It seems essential to establish performance standards for every type of building and the designer's job is to satisfy these standards, which are based upon measurement. All this rests upon a dreadful fallacy because what people want in architecture is *not a stable element*. Whatever they are given will condition them not to like what they are given but to grow tired of it, just as they grow tired of one fashion in clothes and seek something new. This, of course, is a terrible thing to say in the context of the "modern movement", but fashion is and must be recognised as being an enormously powerful force. The techniques of art history and archaeology are based upon the fact that taste changes and the artifacts of the past record, with remarkable precision, the date of manufacture. So we are concerned with a constant state of *change* in which the next condition is unpredictable. This being so "performance standards" will also have to change; the ideal of one decade may be the anathema of the next. So the best that the environmental scientists can do (and it is well worth doing) is to formulate specific environmental conditions and establish the means of achieving them and the means of checking whether they have been achieved. This is really an improvement of the means of specification, but a specification has to take account of the infinitely variable taste of the client and the constant state of flux in opinion about relative values.

So far we have considered art, architecture and functionalism in a somewhat conventional way, leaving out major social and economic influences. Mankind entered the twentieth century equipped with architecture built by craftsmen and with a population of about two thousand million people. The population has now doubled and the material standard of living in what are called "the developed countries" has risen enormously. Manufacture, that is the making of things by *hand*, has largely given way to *machinafacture*,[14] in which the human labour component is reduced to a minimum. In the heroic era of the "modern movement" Morris and Ghandi looked fuddy-duddy and the machine-tool was thought to be the passport to human liberation. Experience has revealed the fact that man does not want to be liberated from work. He is naturally creative and has the peculiarity of being an improving animal but, unfortunately, work which was inevitable in the past has remained the means by which he earns a living in an industrialised society. If we are to reap the benefits of the technological revolution we must separate work from wages.[15]

As living standards have risen so has the cost of labour. Population is still increasing and the need for labour is diminishing. This should mean that we have ample time in which to do and make things which are enjoyable, but we are inhibited by an out-of-date economic system, and though we are richer than men have ever been, and can execute operations which our ancestors would have regarded as miraculous, we "cannot afford" embellishment, decoration and luxury in our buildings. We are prisoners of an economic system which makes us study cost-effectiveness and pursue cheapness, which makes us extravagant with materials which are becoming scarce and economical with labour which is plentiful to excess. We regard money as a precious *commodity* instead of treating it as a convenient means of exchange.

But other factors have tended towards a progressive cheapening of architecture and not least the reasonable argument that, in a world where so many millions of people are living in squalor, resources should be deployed as economically as possible. So we have pressure from the money-merchants for low cost and maximum profit and, from the other side, people with a social conscience are likewise demanding maximum social value for money spent. Modern architecture, with its functional basis, its cult of expressing the structure, which in ninety per cent of cases is no more than a simple grid, and its abstract aesthetic which gives artistic sanction to arrangements of rectangles faintly echoing some of the paintings of Mondrian, is conveniently susceptible to the process of cheapening. The work of certain masters such as Mies van der Röhe and Arne Jacobsen is far from cheap and embodies extremely high standards of finish and indeed of hand craftsmanship, though this fact is not obvious to the layman. But if one does not look too closely the general stylistic effect can be emulated with poor standards of material and finish. This modern *pastiche* is the profit-making formula of the business architect.

The end of World War Two provided the opportunity for modern architecture to be exploited as a style. It was relatively cheap and easy to erect. A new kind of organisation came into being for creating such buildings—the big architects' offices, the consortia, the apparatus of big business with integrated skills and services and so-called economies of scale. In some offices design standards were maintained at a fairly high level but a great deal of architecture in the neo-modern style is produced by organisation rather than design. Such organisation favours neither originality nor finesse and, unhappily, it is seen at its worst in the more socially responsible organisations with their low salaries which do not attract enough people who will fight to achieve architecture in spite of the system.

# chapter 3
# Whose Fault?

In the hot-house atmosphere of a school of architecture, or in the committee rooms of a professional institute, it is only too easy to be infected with the belief that architects control the social climate in which they work. One is prone to take the biographies of the masters of modern architecture at their face value and see the architect as a god-like being or a priest who holds the secrets of an arcane mystery. Being the guardian of a beneficent cult which the uninitiated must not question, the architect is conscious of his superior nature and his mission to mould the environment for the good of mankind. In the hard world of commercial practice this vision quickly fades into the light of common day but the architects, and their assistants, have learned a way of design which tends to stay with them for the rest of their lives because only a few are capable of developing beyond their level of achievement on graduation. It is thus that the general level of architectural practice tends to reflect the kind of design that was current in the schools of architecture some twenty years earlier. And if we ask where this kind of design came from the answer has been the same for generations of architects right back to the middle ages. The trend has been set by a small number of particularly sensitive men who have been able, in their maturity, to respond to changing conditions of which, in many cases, they were probably not consciously aware. The great artist, and I use that word deliberately in referring to such architects as Brunelleschi, François Mansart, Wren, Street, and Frank Lloyd Wright, is above all things *sensitive* to the wind of change, but he is an interpreter, an explorer, not an originator outside the practice of his art.

To the distress of the more intellectual members of his profession the ordinary architect does not learn by theory but by assimilation, imitation and adaptation and this is a fact which we must accept. Like the musician, the architect has to have a special kind of mind without which success is virtually impossible. The architectural mind has a special capacity for absorbing and synthesising. It is a sensitive, responding mind which is capable of originating archi-

15

tecture but is rarely creative in other ways. It is much more intuitive than philosophical and feeds upon relationships rather than ideas. For example, all the related activities inherent in the problem of building a house are resolved in terms of formal and structural relationships. But when the architect begins to move out from his own special skill and tell people what *kind* of houses they ought to live in he is in peril of making a fool of himself. None the less, the temptation to do so is strong because the architect's special qualities of mind make it possible for him to imagine designs which are responses to imaginary conditions. Sydney Opera House is one of the more extreme examples of the architectural imagination "licentiously flying out"[1] from the realities of the problem.

There is a long history of uninhibited architectural imagination. We find it in medieval and Renaissance paintings, in Piranesi, in Boullée and in that great tradition of architecture-abstracted-from-reality which we call "Beaux Arts". The modern movement had roots in revolutionary philosophy and in Art Nouveau. It encouraged the architect to re-think not only his response to the problems of designing architecture, but also to re-think and re-define the problems themselves. Here again, Le Corbusier brings the movement into sharp focus. He was not only an artist but also tried to be a social philosopher. As an artist he was great, but his re-thinking of the social and human problems was experimental, often naïve, and sometimes disastrous in its consequences. He was, indeed, essentially a Beaux Arts architect working in a new idiom but, in the true tradition of the Beaux Arts school, giving himself an ideal programme which was conditioned by his predilection for a way of solving it. If you want to design a transparent house, or a house on stilts, or a city of towers, it is easy to fabricate a case for doing so if you suppress the reasons for not doing so. Likewise, in town planning, which has sprung from architecture and inherited its malignant introversion, there are plenty of excuses for beguiling yourself into believing that what you want to do is what ought to be done.

We are back to *the treason of the artists*. Architects have come to it by a different route but, like so many painters and sculptors, they have separated themselves from reality. In times of social disruption, disorder, and disquiet, the sensitive mind may retreat from reality into fantasy or into abstraction.[2] An alternative is to identify oneself with what one hates. This kind of devil-worship is a common phenomenon manifested in the witches' sabbath, the black mass, sadism, masochism and in art as the representation of beastliness and ugliness, not infrequently with hypocritical moral overtones. In architecture some aspects of Mannerism and Art Nouveau, belong with this cult of the flowers of evil and the modern version seems to be Brutalism—we live in a brutal and insensitive age so let our architecture be brutal too.

Abstraction, Fantasy, Brutalism; we have them all—escape and cynicism, but in the past such movements have been short-lived. Some artists, in any period, are likely to tend towards fantasy on the one hand and often to masochism and expressionism on the other, and there may be great ones among them; but in our time the edges have closed in towards the centre, like a diseased leaf, and the main body of artists has rejected mankind. The architects have gone along with them.

This may seem a surprising and even a malicious statement to the many architects who have a deep sense of social responsibility and devote themselves to such tasks as slum clearance; but look at the results! If the salt has lost its savour wherewith shall it be salted? And there are many artists on the political Left; but how far is this a new orthodoxy? A political commitment to an ideology which is thought to be beneficial for mankind is quite, quite different from an artistic commitment to mankind. The one is an easily acquired mental attitude, the other is a deep emotional involvement, a care for and faith in Man.

The "modern movement" is ending in cynicism, escapism and rejection. If we are to recapture sympathy and concern for people and reality we must escape from the cloud-cuckoo land of art for its own sake, of art with its own internal and unrelated value-system. This means that we must see art in its social context, not as an embellishment but as an integral and essential part of life, not as the ring on the finger but as the love it represents.

To do this we have to bring the artist down off his pedestal and ask him to accept the reasonable fact that he is one kind of person among people of many kinds who are mostly worthy of respect. He is necessary and important; not a luxury, a refinement, nor, for that matter, a drop-out. But to establish the reality of the artist among us we have to give definition to his rôle in society. For the architect, and it is with architects that we are concerned in this book, the first requirement is that we should delineate the respective rôles of the architect, his patron or client, and the people who share the environment to which both architect and client contribute.

The architect does not make the society in which he works. He does not set the problems which he has to solve, and we have seen something of the danger of the architect generating the conditions to which he is to respond. All art is a two-way traffic. It does not occur in isolation but is generated by relationships. If we complain of the quality of most contemporary architecture it is unfair simply to blame the architects: we must look at the other side of the equation. If we isolate the architect as the man with a special kind of brain, and with skill in responding to the problems of creating an environment for people, as a man with a particular service to give, or sell, to society, we must consider the other side and question the means by which he is employed.

Paradoxically and foolishly, but understandably, architects have tried, to some extent, to put society right in order that they might produce better architecture. But the architect can only hope to participate effectively in social and political amelioration by ceasing to be an architect. If he tries to be on both sides of the equation at the same time he will simply cancel himself out. The architect is not in control of the conditions in which he must work. If he has to work in outrageous conditions, as the modern architect does, he can hardly be blamed for trying to set things right, but in doing so he is like the peasant who joins a revolutionary army and dies on the battlefield. The architect, like all other artists, craftsmen and tradesmen, is dependent upon patronage, and if we are really to get to the roots of the contemporary decline in architectural quality we must look at the quality of the patronage. This is deplorable. The time has come for architects to stop covering-up for their clients and state unequivocally that the practice of architecture is becoming impossible. It is therefore a social necessity, not just the responsibility of architects, to alter the conditions under which architects are employed. In short, architects have tried to adjust themselves to social conditions in which environmental standards are being continuously debased—and this is true everywhere, no matter what the political flavour of the government may be.

In a situation which necessitates a revolution the best contribution architects can make is to state clearly the values for which they stand *as architects*; in other words to say, "*Architecture is a fine and beautiful thing. It is concerned with the quality of the environment in which we all live. If you want to enrich your lives by living in convenient and beautiful places we are the people with the skills to create such places.*" The first question then to be asked is whether the claim to have the skills is true. At present it is *not*, and this is a matter for architects themselves to put right by concentrating upon it instead of dissipating themselves in all sorts of activities for which they are quite incompetent. The next thing to be said is that architects must "stick to their last" and not squander their energies in promoting social policies. But if architects accept the fact that architecture is far too big and fascinating a subject ever to be comprehended by any one man in a single lifetime, a subject to which dedication is a delight, they must consequently acquiesce in the sharing of architectural responsibility with patrons and public. Architects do not, and cannot, create the social climate in which they have to work. Other people must share the responsibility for architecture; indeed this is probably true of all the arts. A society gets the art it deserves. The responsibility cannot be hived off: it rests upon the whole of society and that society's political, social and economic institutions. Art, in fact, is the responsibility, and in a sense, the reflected image of everyone, not just the artists. Artists are dependents, not demi-gods. The best public service an architect can do is to uphold and exemplify in his work the value of architecture. By dissipating themselves in other activities, no matter how important these may seem to be for the practice of architecture, the architects weaken themselves. To succeed they must make architecture central and look out from it. By this I mean that they can properly and usefully proclaim what architecture has to offer to society. It is essential that they should be able to provide that quality in practice which they proclaim in principle. The ultimate test of architects is the quality of what they design and build. The quality of a civilization is reflected in what society encourages and allows architects to design and build.[3]

To be effective as an architect one must stay on one side of the equation and here I must explain that I myself, though "qualified" as an architect, have ceased to be one by virtue of the fact that I have moved over onto the other side to involve myself in the study of architecture as a phenomenon: its history, its relationship and value to society, its status as an art in relation to other arts, its ecological and philosophical implications. This change-over was a conscious and premeditated step in my life which was not taken without some regrets. I have moved, if I may change the metaphor, from an inside to an outside position—outside the practice of architecture. It would have been foolish to think that I could be outside and remain inside and I moved deliberately because that was necessary for what I wanted to do. It is perhaps, an advantage that I was, for a time on the inside during a period when the practice of architecture was undergoing rapid change.[4]

The biggest change has been in the decline of private individual patronage, which sustained a personal relationship between architect and client. Almost equally important have been the decline (and in many countries the almost complete cessation) of large-scale private domestic building and of religious building. Only fifty years ago churches and private houses offered a great variety of artistic scope to architects. And there was civic architecture, in which the Town Hall still had a respected symbolic character before it became a municipal office and the stronghold of a bureaucracy.

Generally architects worked for individuals, with whom there could be personal communion, or for identifiable corporate bodies which had a well-understood significance. Under such conditions most of the best architecture stemming from the Arts and Crafts Movement as well as many of the significant pioneer buildings of the "modern movement" were designed.

Having said this I must emphasise that by identifying what has happened one does not necessarily decry the social changes which have brought about new conditions under which architects have to work. By saying that private patronage has declined I am *not* advocating a return to the social conditions of the nineteen-twenties. By saying that the town hall has ceased to be a respectable symbol I am *not* condoning the ludicrous pomp of local government institutions which still lingers with us, nor am I approving the present growth of municipal bureaucracy. By pointing to the scarcity of opportunities to design churches I am *not* wishing for a revival of Victorian Christianity. Furthermore, by identifying modern trends in social organisation which have had an adverse effect upon the practice of architecture I am *not* disapproving of those trends. It is necessary to say these things because we have become so habituated to propaganda and social-political exposition which allows no looking back, or even looking round, but requires every faithful comrade to wear blinkers, that by recognising some good in what we have discarded, and some evil in what we now embrace, I am in some danger of being dismissed as a reactionary.

Only a fool lives entirely in the present, without reference to what has happened in the past or thought for the future. The lesson of the past is that the future will be full of change, not a perpetuation of our present ideas. This is the way of life for human beings and our responsibility is to safeguard for our children and our grandchildren *the right to change things*, not shackle them with immutable institutions or bind them with ideas of eternal rectitude. Thus the purpose of this book is to question, as impartially as may be, the orthodoxy of modern architecture, not with nostalgia but with an eye to improvement and change in the future.

Patronage has changed and the architect serves new masters. The money for building comes from two main sources, namely, public funds and finance houses. According to whether a country's government leans towards socialism or capitalism the one or the other predominates.

It is valid, though unorthodox (because "capital" is a dirty word for socialists) to describe socialism as a system in which all capital is owned by the people and administered by the state which is conceived to be their democratically elected government. All building requires capital investment and the use of land. In theory a socialist society should be able to deploy resources so as to produce an idyllic environment—provided that the people want, and are effectively represented by a government which wants, the best that architects can give them. The evidence "on the ground" suggests that socialist societies still have a long way to go before they can begin to compete with, for example, ancient Priene, medieval Cologne or renaissance Bar le Duc.

In the context of modern political and social dispute Britain is a fascinating laboratory. It has achieved a high *material* standard in buildings for housing and education by the appropriation of very substantial resources for these purposes. Very little indeed of the vast amount of money spent has resulted in admirable architecture though it has produced accommodation which, by world standards, is good. The British "council house" is a dwelling which is enviable by the standards of ninety per cent of the world's population. It is generally considered to be uneconomic and ironically it is available only to a privileged minority who happen to be in the right place at the right time. (Most privileged minorities come about in this way!)

Generally the effect of bureaucracy upon architecture is to assert the standards of people who have never had the opportunity to know better upon the people who want homes. This comes about partly because so many public servants are just one generation up from the old working class standards, from slums, poverty and poor educational facilities. Time will change this. It is unwise to expect the full effects of education in one generation. But while we may reasonably believe that socialisation will lead to progressive improvement in material standards it would also appear that the channelling of architectural patronage through a bureau-

cratic system, serving the community through committees of
elected representatives, is more likely to foster mediocrity than
distinction.[5] The cure for this must lie in raising standards within
the architectural profession, in architects asserting and exemplify-
ing the value of good design, and, no less, in those who care
about architecture playing their part in education, in public
discussion about architecture, in thinking and writing about
architecture and in making environmental issues matters of
lively public concern. In other words, I am saying again that the
impetus must come from inside architecture, out to society.
Architects must believe in architecture and contribute it to the
society in which they work. If, instead of working through architecture, they try to alter society (although this may, by other
standards, be an admirable thing) they are ceasing to be architects.[6] There is probably much to be said for having some politicians and administrators who have been architects but for the
individual architect this status would, in each case, involve a
change of vocation.

Socialism, and bureaucracy whether it is serving a democratic
or a totalitarian regime, present a particular kind of problem in
that, while they may seem beneficially to provide the means for
designing the human environment sensibly, they generate a
problem of how to liberate the necessary talent. Private patronage
in a free economy, on the other hand, is claimed to do this very
thing; in the past that claim may have been justified, but vast
changes have taken place in financial organisation within the
capitalist system. Finance has become an industry on its own
and whereas the capitalist system used to be based upon the
availability in the open market of "risk capital" this is rapidly
ceasing to be the case. Money for "development" is now largely
administered by financiers who are actuated purely by the desire
for profit. Their industry is the profitable administration of money.
There have, of course, been bankers for many centuries and they
served and continue to serve a useful purpose. They had, in the
past, the power to sustain or break monarchies, to finance wars
and develop trade but their power was never anything like that
which they wield at present. One reason for this is the growth of
insurance to the extent that most prudent people "lay off"
most of the financial hazards that are not covered by state welfare
(and some which are, as an additional precaution). In a risk-
taking capitalist society it has now become normal for individuals
and institutions to insure against risks and for anticipated liabili-
ties such as education and retirement.[7] Thus enormous sums of

money pass to insurance companies which invest these monies as profitably as possible. Investment in existing shares would merely push up the price of the shares out of all proportion to what they represent in industrial equipment and output so, apparently very properly, new fields for creative investment are sought. This ought to mean that money is available for all kinds of desirable enterprise; *but it doesn't*. At one end of the scale the overhead costs, greatly inflated by the financial fatness of the industry, seemingly inhibit the consideration of investment in small enterprises and profitability is the one criterion which is applied, whereas the capitalist system in the past achieved many of its most spectacular successes by long term investment in highly risky ventures. In one field alone, the building societies, is finance readily available on a small scale and even here the architectural thinking of the building societies is notoriously reactionary, hostile to innovation and outrageously prejudiced against old property no matter how architecturally valuable. At the other end of the scale very large sums of money are available for "comprehensive redevelopment" which is easy to administer and provides a large, tidy financial package. Thus the financiers foster and sustain the kind of "thinking big" which tears out the hearts of old cities regardless of character, tradition, sense of place and all other values save only rent per square metre of accommodation.

The awful price we pay for insuring against risks is the progressive enrichment of insurance companies. The initiative for investing in architecture is passing to these companies and their financial subsidiaries whose only criterion is profitability. The men in power are professional financiers and accountants but they are not accountable to society. They are under no control other than that of their own boards of directors and they are often aided and abetted by the very government authorities, local and national, which administer the laws devised to protect the environment. It is not easy, even for the most honest and dedicated of planning officers, to turn down an "investment" of millions of pounds in the centre of his city or even in its green belt. Public opinion, in many cases, would not support him.

There is a widespread belief among rich people that the possession of money carries with it no responsibility for the use of that money, and unhappily we have enormous sums of money available for investment in architecture, and the environment, but it is irresponsibly and, by every other standard except profitability, incompetently administered. A searchlight needs to be turned upon the financiers: unless they can put their house in order the time must come when they will suffer the same fate as the monasteries did in England under Henry VIII and in France during the revolution; and for the same reason, that they are corporate bodies which do not die and gradually acquire, simply by continuing to exist, too large a share of the nation's land and property. Unless something is done everything will eventually belong to the insurance companies. That is a matter of simple arithmetic.

So under advanced, institutionalised modern capitalism we have far more frustration and much more unsuitable administration and disposition of funds for architecture than any capitalist has ever envisaged as being the inevitable outcome of socialism!

We began this chapter with the question "Whose fault?" The answer is not simple. At the heart of it there is the incompetence, disunity and lack of dedication of many architects; their lack of faith in their trade; and the dissipation of their activities in either trying to accommodate themselves to what their masters want or attempting to reform the system of society in the interests of architecture. There is the treason of the architects, their selling of the pass by denying the value of what they are, by denying the value of architecture. If architects do not believe in architecture how can they expect other people to do so? By lack of faith they betray society to the growing and dangerous power of mere technologists who have no standards other than brute functionalism.

But the despair which makes many able young architects turn away from architecture is a rational response to outrageous conditions in society. Whether one looks politically to the left or to the right the current policies are leading to progressive deterioration of the environment. One wonders whether it will be on the left or the right, or from somewhere in the middle, that the new lead will come in recognition of the fact that the old shibboleths of social debate and economic dispute are irrelevant if, by either route, we are all to achieve equality by living together in one midden.

# chapter 4
# What has happened?

The modern movement in architecture has been intensely self-conscious. It has been advanced by minorities, by groups of great diversity which have all been crammed into the portmanteau of the movement. The background was the modern movement in painting with its coteries of artists attracted to the nucleus of a single master or joined in allegiance to an idea or theory. Adherence to the modern movement became a qualification for membership in an international club which included a hard core of original designers and thinkers together with a growing, and ultimately corrupting, majority of opportunists who were prepared to design in any style their clients might want but saw advantages in commitment to the modern movement and a "modern style". There was no overall theory but, by implication, modern architecture was not a style; it was "the evolution of a final type or norm, whose perfection, he (Le Corbusier), Pierre Urbaine, Paul Valéry, Piet Mondrian and many others saw as an event of the immediate future, or even the immediate past".[1] Even Gropius spoke of the need for a modern style and he seems to have meant a permanent international norm. But style implies change, implies fashion, and what most of the modernists were claiming was a right to establish norms for all time. They did not see themselves as incidents in the long pageant of architecture which is a reflection of humanity. They saw the end of artistic evolution and the establishment of the correct architecture for ever. Whatever their political complexion most members of the movement accepted a deterministic view of history which saw the future in terms of the imperfections of the present, and closed its eyes to the possibility that generations to come might have new and better ideas from which new, and currently inconceivable, lines of development might arise.

Up to the outbreak of the Second World War in 1939 the effect of the modern movement upon the actual practice of architecture had been slight. Most buildings were traditional, with small stylistic concessions to modernism. Italy and Germany, under

25

fascist régimes, had committed themselves to a version of the
inhuman monumentality of Futurism as expressed by Sant' Elia,
the dominance of an élite-controlled environment over the
individuality of man. The abdication of Gropius from the Bauhaus
in 1928 and the dispersal, mainly into English-speaking countries,
of the men of genius who had congregated there, paved the way
for the triumph, as it seemed, of the modern movement in the
post-war years when even the buildings of the United Nations
and UNESCO were entrusted to *committees* of modern architects.
In a Europe where resources were scarce and the need for re-
building was urgent, austerity and economy favoured the plain-
ness of modernism and the idea of functionalism was slightly
twisted to provide a theoretical justification for solving architectural problems in the *cheapest* way.[2] The cheapest way of
providing what was necessary became the norm for housing,
schools, universities, factories and most other types of building.
It was proper to despise luxurious building at a time when so
much needed to be done to repair the ravages of war and make
good the neglect of architectural replacement in the war
years.

Meanwhile a new impetus had been given to the study of
architectural history. It stemmed in part from the intellectual
dispersal which was precipitated by the Nazi revolution in
Germany. Nikolaus Pevsner brought the pragmatic techniques
of German art-historical scholarship, and a profound nostalgia
for Europe[3] to England and wrote a book which was to become,
for readers in the English language, the most potent rationalisa-
tion of a view of the modern movement. It was called *Pioneers of
the Modern Movement.*[4]

Pevsner, and to a lesser extent Sigfried Giedion, brought to
the modern movement the authority of Germanic art-historical
scholarship. They both endorsed the movement as historically
important and, one may think, forfeited their right to consideration
as serious historians of it by committing themselves, thus becoming propagandists and campaigners.

It is the common fate of important scholarly studies, which by
rare fortune attract wide public notice, to be understood by the
generality of people in speciously simplistic terms. Reduced to
common understanding Pevsner's *Pioneers of the Modern Movement* meant that the modern movement had started in England
with Morris and reaction against the design standards of the
1851 Exhibition. Art Nouveau had shown the way towards new
form and had gained recognition in Europe but England, the

pioneer of the industrial revolution, had failed to detach itself from an obsession with hand-craftsmanship and the initiative had passed to Germany, culminating in the Bauhaus and the creation of industrial prototypes for a machine age.

But in fact Walter Gropius was a true heir to the Arts and Crafts Movement and was well aware that the creation of prototypes depends upon hand-craftsmanship, which was the basis of the Bauhaus training. Indeed in his 1919 Manifesto Gropius wrote: "Let us create a new guild of craftsmen without the class-snobbery that tries to erect a haughty barrier between artist and craftsman. Let us conceive, consider and create together the new building of the future that will bring all into one single integrated creation: painting and sculpture rising to Heaven out of the hands of a million craftsmen, the crystal symbol of the new faith of the future."

No Master of the Art Workers Guild in London could have expressed the aims of the Arts and Crafts Movement more truly, but Gropius was only saying what masters of that Guild had been saying in inaugural addresses for the previous thirty years. One of them, W. R. Lethaby, had gone much further in thinking about the nature of architecture and art in the modern world yet, by a curious distortion, he has been omitted from the legend of the modern movement. The Bauhaus Manifesto of 1919 proclaimed the ideals of the Art Workers Guild in England but there was a difference, and in the climate of the last fifty years it has seemed to be a beneficial difference. The Bauhaus moved, despite formidable difficulties, towards the use of hand-craftsmanship for the creation of prototypes for machine-made objects and in the process bowed down to the then fashionable worship of technology. Simplistically stated, hand tools are bad; machine tools are good. It was the first machine age. Machines were wonderful and architects, for no discernible reason, had to get onto the mechanised bandwagon.

The great illusion of the first machine age was that man must accommodate himself to machinery, that he must design for the machine and that mechanical engineering could establish aesthetic standards. Since then there has been a revolution in machinery. Mechanistic expressionism—which was congenial to German artists and thinkers[5]—gave way to aerodynamic design, pioneered in the motor and aircraft industries, which spread as a fashion to immobile objects. Machinery acquired a skin and then an electronic nervous system. The expressionist engineering of early automobiles and aircraft which Le Corbusier admiringly illustrated in *Vers une Architecture* now have a quaint charm like half-timbered manor houses of the sixteenth century.

But an even more important change is the one to be seen in the growing recognition that technology must be brought under ecological control. Traffic congestion, aircraft noise, atmospheric pollution, the sheer destructive power of machinery and the hideous absurdity of the hydrogen bomb have soured the flavour of a mechanistic aesthetic. Furthermore, the true effects of mass production are becoming apparent and the romantic notions of the 'thirties are dissolving as we realise that, by standardising the production of a wide range of useful appliances and commodities, we actually create a demand for the unique or rare object which raises the prices of antiques of almost every kind to astonishing levels. Mass products will not be the antiques of the future and many of them are currently designed and made with built-in obsolescence in order to keep the machines employed and the factory workers in their jobs. Antiques will not be able to satisfy the demand and there is an immense potential market for works of hand-craftsmanship. Unfortunately the art schools are still, for the most part, sunk in the slough of the old modern movement and it will take time to recover standards of craftsmanship and design by craftsmen, such as Gropius advocated in 1919. He was right and so were Morris, Lethaby, C. F. A. Voysey and a host of others who have been regarded for some years as the failures of the movement because they were not bewitched by the machine.

*Automation must now be seen as liberating the creative mind and hands of the craftsman.* The labour-saving devices and standardised parts from which building technique can now benefit must not be mistaken for architecture. The economic problem will be solved by the pressure of demand based upon the mounting need of people for beauty, decoration, individuation and objects of significance. The immediate problem is to resurrect craftsmanship in the art schools and sweep out the rubbish of art which is mere self-expression, or posturing for the admiration of some artistic coven.

The history of art should never be considered in isolation from the history of man because art is a part of life, not the whole; and it can only exist as a part, never on its own. The difficulty of knowing enough to see art as an aspect of human history is no excuse for pretending that it can be studied in isolation; this applies with special force to the history of the modern movement in architecture. For our present purpose it is necessary to consider three potent influences from outside upon art. These are the defeat of Germany in the two world wars, the idea of progress so dear to Victorian Englishmen, and the phenomenon of socialism. Each of these is a vast subject in itself and, at the risk of appearing extremely simplistic, I must, in the present context, draw attention to powerful influences upon architecture without examining or explaining them in detail.

When Rome conquered Greece in the second century B.C. it is arguable that the Romans won the war and the Greeks won the peace by the cultural conquest of Rome. A comparison with Germany and the Western Allies is interesting. The first Bauhau. Manifesto dates from 1919, one year after the defeat of Germany, Walter Gropius has become so much an international figures detached from Germany by his detestation of the Nazis, his emigration to England and his professorship at Harvard, that we tend to forget he was a German cavalry officer, with a family background in Brunswick, and deep roots in the social and intellectual life of Germany. The First World War can be seen as a confrontation between countries whose artistic heritage derived largely from Italy and the High Renaissance, and countries of eastern Europe which received classical influences mainly at the Baroque stage of development. There was less of formal classicism and more of expressionism in the German empire. The curious phenomenon of Richard Wagner and his strange cycle of operas, *The Ring*, culminating in the triumph of evil, and *The Twilight of the Gods* was hauntingly relevant to the collapse of the Kaiser's imperial ambitions and the humiliation of the fatherland. It was even more relevant to Hitler. Through the Bauhaus, German influence spread to all the progressive schools of art and architecture, carrying with it the seeds of expressionism. Many influences have shaped the subsequent development of expressionism throughout the world, not least popular versions of Freudian psychology, and the irony of it all lies in the fact that personal self-expression has become dominant in the thinking of so many art students, and their teachers, that the craft side of the message of the Bauhaus has been neglected.[6]

The idea of progress was especially dear to people in the nineteenth century. Between 1850 and 1880, despite the warnings of a farsighted minority, there was abundant evidence to support the idea that science and technology, together with progress in the study of the liberal arts, would create a continuously improving condition of mankind upon earth. The architectural counterpart of this faith in progress is interesting: when it was at its highest, architecture emphasised links with the past and sought to bring together, by allusion, all the reassuring and stabilising achievements from the cultures of the past. Victorian architecture in England truly reflected a progressive society which could enjoy the comfort of an architecture of allusion to the past. In astonishing contrast, modern architecture coincides with disillusion and loss of faith in "progress". We may observe that the missionary quality of modern architecture lapsed after World War Two when speed of erection and cheapness favoured it. Upon this utilitarian basis it has prospered and for the public the meaning of modern architecture is all too often, quite simply, expedience, speed and cheapness. But looking deeper we may suspect that modern architects' obsession with *progressive* architecture is a pathetic late reaction to the conditions of the nineteenth rather than the mid-twentieth century.[7]

"Socialism is a body of teaching and practice resting upon the belief that most social evils are due to excessively unequal distribution of material resources; and that these evils can be cured only by the transference, gradual or immediate, total or partial, of the ownership of property and of the means of production and distribution from private to public control." This definition, by Sir Isiah Berlin,[8] underlines the intellectual side of socialism at the expense of both the compassion which moves people to wish to relieve hardships of the underprivileged and the resentment of the underprivileged themselves as a political force. It is right to exclude these considerations: concern for the underprivileged is not exclusive to socialists, and resentment does not always clamour for a socialist solution. On the other hand, much of the impetus for reform has come from the left, even when the action has come from the right, and an important ingredient in socialism has been the demand for better living and working conditions. Socialist thinking has had a profound effect upon architecture, quite apart from all the artistic trends which are lumped together in the modern movement. Yet socialism has, in fact, done very little for architecture and so far the emphasis has been, quite understandably, utilitarian. Many people are now becoming aware that the utilitarian solutions of today are producing new slums, like the slums that resulted from utilitarian thinking in the nineteenth century but with an additional disadvantage, for a horizontal slum street laid out on the surface of the earth is better than a vertical slum street with its constant invitation to suicide. A room with a view is a poor place for a family if it has lost contact with the earth. The lesson seems to be that socialism without imaginative sympathy for people is in danger of substituting one evil for another. There is a real problem of quality in a socialist society and in the next chapter it will be necessary to digress from our main theme to consider this briefly insofar as it affects architecture.

The pattern of the modern movement was exceedingly complex and some of its elements were fiercely discordant with others. In the Bauhaus itself there were deep scisms: Gropius's belief in the value of hand-craftsmanship as an educational discipline, Itten's basic course, functionalism, the machine aesthetic and the strange automated, de-humanised expressionism revealed in the *Triadic Ballet*. There were also the explosive stresses created by the coming together of so many individualistic artists of genius around this small bright place in the post-war darkness. But the Bauhaus, though important, is a small component in the modern movement which, in its later phases, was to come under the spell of Le Corbusier. Meanwhile Futurism, De Stijl, and the later manifestations of Art Nouveau and the Arts and Crafts Movement, especially in Frank Lloyd Wright, together with the American dream of mass production leading to technical mastery of the world and the growth of the welfare state, especially in Britain, all played their part.

But a tremendous amount was left out and a curious aspect of the modern movement is indicated by the publisher's description of *A History of Modern Architecture* by Jürgen Joedicke[9] as: "The first general history of the *modern movement* in architecture . . ." (my italics). It is as though one were to write the history of modern politics and leave out communism. The modern movement is not the whole of modern architecture but there has been a conspiracy to exclude from history that which does not seem to come within the scope of what modernists approved. The same thing has happened in other arts: the word *modern* has been appropriated by a loose and disparate association of people who think of themselves as "the moderns", thereby implying that all others are old-fashioned. But in a historical sense the old-fashioned are just as much modern as the avant-garde. When the history of twentieth-century art and architecture comes to be written there will probably be some major revaluations. Vincent Harris and Le Corbusier will be seen as contemporaries, likewise Lutyens, Frank Lloyd Wright and C. R. Mackintosh who were all born in 1869. Historical evaluations will depend upon what happens in the future.

This idea of modernism as something exclusive to an élite among artists is pernicious and astonishingly at variance with both the expressionist and the socialist elements in twentieth-century art. If an artist has a unique vision, an original response to life and the environment or, more likely, to some tiny facet of it, so that he is able to perceive a small but unique and important truth, it is an outrageous critical tyranny that he should be required to conform to an idiom of presentation which is currently regarded as "modern" (See below, p. 74 the total view of art).

It may be, and I think it is true, that in painting and sculpture the little groups which have furthered a particular way of working, usually within the inspiration of a single master-practitioner or a single sectarian theory about art, have achieved something valuable in the evolution of art in the last hundred years. But the painter and sculptor, if they so choose, can be independent of the public, can work for themselves alone or for the admiration of their friends; architects, on the other hand, work for people, for all people, producing the homes they live in and the public or religious buildings which symbolise and provide for their beliefs about life. It is a tragedy that modern architecture has become embroiled in little sectarian movements of a purely artistic kind which ignore the people for whom architecture is built. Art history has done a disservice to architecture and to humanity by glorifying individualistic, élitist and sectarian cults in architectural design. The job of the historian is to understand and explain what happened, not to say what ought to happen in terms of the categorisations which are part of his professional technique.

The modern movement comprises a multiplicity of artistic clubs and theories, but the outstanding characteristic of the movement—a characteristic which will make it appear as an aberration in the total history of architecture—is the overwhelming concern of the modernists with *themselves* and their theories, their disregard of what real people, other than themselves, want in the way of architecture. I believe that architecture is an art, but its artistic merit has been jeopardised by modernists who have conducted a self-interested campaign to appropriate art for their own purposes and deprive the people of an essential part of life.[10]

To guess what historians of the future will think about our time is rash indeed but even so I would suggest that a verdict is emerging. What its members thought of as "The Modern Movement" (with capital letters) never happened. The period 1919 to 1970 is characterised by a multiplicity of competing experiments and may properly be called *Twentieth-Century Transitional*. It may be seen to have paved the way for an architecture which belongs to the humanity of modern civilization.

# chapter 5
# Quality and Education

Only the most obtuse of men and women can have failed to
become aware that a revolution in thinking about the nature
of society has taken place. These obscurantists cling to the old
habits of evaluation. Yet among those who are aware of the
consequences of social policies which have gone some distance
towards realising the ideals of socialism, there is still a great deal
of reluctance to abandon ways of thought and habits of value
judgement which belong properly to an alien and élitist form of
society. People who condemn élitism are all too often unconsciously caught in its spells. This is nowhere more apparent than
in education which has been seen both as a tool for eliminating
privilege, by giving the same opportunities to all children, and
at the same time as a means of giving them equal opportunities
to get on in the world by differentiating themselves at the start
of "the rat race" towards "meritocracy".[1] Hence the growing
suspicion of higher education, and especially universities, with a
compensating, self-defensive rejection by intellectuals of what
they call *élitism*. The paradox arises from mistakes on both sides:
on one, regarding education as a means towards "equality"
of people (in the spirit of the declaration that all men are born
equal); on the other, the desire of underprivileged parents to
use education as the means whereby their children may become
privileged. Both attitudes belong to, and have come no further
than, enlightened thinking in the eighteenth century. It is therefore not surprising that architects likewise remain obsessed by
ideas which have been overtaken by realities of modern society.

In the late eighteenth century revolution was in the consciousness of most men, either as a terror or as the supposed gateway
to a fairer world. Society was stratified with a wealthy élite
sustained by the ownership of land, a relatively small prosperous
middle class based upon trade, a large number of peasants
and poorly paid workers. Between the middle and upper class
there was a small but highly creative group of artists and intellectuals, tenuously linked to universities with deep ecclesiastical

traditions, sustained by endowments, small private incomes and patronage. The standards of architecture were derived from Renaissance Italy and had developed in France and England with a curious mixture of rationalism and conservatism, best typified in Lord Burlington's earnest propagation and establishment of Palladianism. This had been done in what was the characteristic pattern of the eighteenth century by the employment (patronage) of talented and educated men without estate, namely William Kent, Giacomo Leoni, the translator of Palladio and Alberti, and Colin Campbell, the compiler of *Vitruvius Britannicus*. The rules of taste and of manners were set by leaders of the aristocracy who were guided by writers, architects, scholars and artists of talent and reasonably submissive temperament. But if we look behind this effective partnership of aristocracy and talent we find that the sources of creation were the men of talent: Palladio, Inigo Jones, Serlio, François Mansart and many other relatively poor men; the aristocrats were the entrepreneurs! This is true right back to that astute banker, Cosimo dei Medici, in the fifteenth century. Before that it had been the Church.

The nineteenth century, and the growth of the mechanical-industrial revolution, had remarkably little effect upon the established order of artistic value judgements. Much more important was the eighteenth-century innovation of the romantic movement and the overturning (most effectively by David Hume) of the Renaissance aesthetic. The industrial *nouveaux riches* aped the manners of what they supposed to be their betters, the established aristocracy, but mostly they failed, as indeed had many aristocrats in the past, to establish any pattern of patronage. Partly as a result of this growth of riches without any sense of cultural obligation, the artists and intellectuals of the nineteenth century were forced into isolation without patronage, the more so in post-revolutionary France where the idea of the "Bohemian" artist, wasting his talent upon the garret air, became archetypal. Despite a few, mostly insincere, genuflections towards the arts, industry and its devotees have failed completely in creative patronage. Concentrating upon profit, industrialists have lit their candles to the deceptive goddess of progress and reluctantly parted with a modicum of the loot under pressure from organised labour backed by new social philosophies. The artists and intellectuals (including the architects under either or both headings) have deserted the paymasters and, in theory at least, aligned themselves with the people. The response of the masters of the new electronic-industrial revolution has been a vast increase in science education to create a new subservient intelligentsia of scientific doctors of philosophy who are dependent upon industrial employment. Art has been bought off by paying vast sums of money for art education which employs artists not to be artists. *If the art schools could be closed and the money diverted to commissioning works of art we could rival and excel the splendours of the Middle Ages or the Renaissance.* Talent awaits opportunity; frustrated, it turns to neuroses.

With this background we still think in terms of class and see education as the means of rising to a higher class. We still have an aristocracy of wealth but its power is precarious because it does not attain respect. Increasingly it appears as an epiphenomenon of a financial swindle of vast proportions, which bestows wealth and the handling of money upon a few people without any apparent justification. It is some consolation that people are beginning to realise that there is no correlation between education and riches. Once this is understood education can start to fulfil its proper rôle of enabling each person to develop his potentialities irrespective of economic gain. *The ideal of a truly egalitarian society should be that everyone may have the opportunity to cultivate their own kind of excellence.*

The current ironic popularity of the dictum that "all men are equal but some are more equal than others"[2] is symptomatic of a deep misunderstanding of what equality means. The illusion persists that only the rich are happy, whereas evidence to the contrary is all around. The illusion persists that the élite must be the people who have power, influence, and wealth—but if we believe in social equality we must learn to recognise that there is not just one élite, a class of people who are different: the "best people", the "bosses", the "creative minority", the "privileged few", the "natural leaders" or simply "the rich". The great and fundamental humane concept is that all men are equal. They must be equal before the law, equal in their rights and equal in their opportunities to live the best lives of which they are capable. *To do this they must be free to differentiate.* Education is a process of differentiation, of cultivation, of bringing out the best that is latent in each human being. This begs the question of what is "best": what is life about and upon what bases do value judgements about living rest. It is not the purpose of this book to attempt an answer to these formidable questions, but it is important to recognise that they exist and that each and every one of us makes an implied attempt to answer them in the way we live. Anyone who has lived for thirty or forty years must know by now that the path divides many times and there are innumerable irreversible choices which have to be made.

The first purpose of education must be to teach us good manners, the basic technique of living with other people; then it must show us the spread of possibilities; then it must help us to evaluate ourselves, to test our powers in different directions and to awaken interests. When a choice of direction has been made it must help us to become excellent, that is to do well what we want to do and as a result of this we become exceptional in our talent. We become specialised. The modern élite are those who do best, in any activity, what others in the same activity do less well, but one cannot see them as a *class* right across the vast field of human activities from motherhood to microscopy. In looking at society in this way we are all ordinary but can take a proper class-less pride in the quality of what we do and our way of life. It is right that distinction should be recognised and admired. The improvement of the human condition, from our present far from satisfactory standards, must depend upon such distinction, but, by being a distinguished practitioner of any activity, occupation or way of life we are not part of an élite because in other respects we are ordinary people.[3]

Returning to architecture: we recognise that design is a special kind of talent which is developed by an architectural education. Architects are differentiated from other people by being architects but they are otherwise ordinary except insofar as they might cultivate other talents. It is not uncommon to find, for example, that a man who excels at tennis or some other secondary activity is a reasonably good architect, a wretched but persistent guitar player, and in all other respects an ordinary citizen. The details may vary but the life-pattern is typical. There are few people who don't take some pride in something they do well: and if they don't they may have reason to complain of their education.

It would be a practical and beneficial ideal of education if it were to enable everyone to do something well. However well we do anything there is room for improvement and change. There seem to be no ultimate attainable standards in anything, perhaps least of all in architecture which is forever beset with compromises; and nobody can be completely satisfied with the excellence of a compromise.

# chapter 6
# The Importance of a Home

A home is not just a building, still less a machine for living in. It is not "a little hut" in isolation no matter how useful that concept may be as a basic aedicule of architecture. The most isolated mountain shepherd's croft is thought of as being on its own because of distance from other dwellings, but over this distance there are links. The shepherd, for example, goes to market. Distance does not detach him from a human community upon which he depends for many physical necessities and even more importantly, for his sense of belonging to a community, to an order of human relationships.

Certainly a home is a place in which to eat and sleep and have one's belongings with some degree of privacy. It is also the place to which one belongs, where one has one's roots. It is more than just a symbol—no matter how simple a cottage or how grand a palace—it is a nest and as such a fundamental necessity to the normal man and woman. Modern psychology has given so much attention to the significance of the copulative side of sex that the equally fundamental nest-building aspect has tended to be overshadowed. Yet the nest, the home, is a necessity both before and after the period of copulative sexual activity. It is fundamental to providing the necessary sense of security for the child and the elderly cling to it, sometimes with desperate tenacity. For lovers it is a coveted goal which is approached through a wilderness of obstructions and technicalities, estate agents, building societies, housing authorities, advisory committees and waiting lists. In modern urban communities we have become dulled to the enormity of consigning people to pigeon holes or forcing them into sharing-arrangements which can have abominable results. So serious are the effects upon people who cannot have a home that one is tempted to wonder whether the copulative side of sex ought not to take second place in our thinking to the satisfaction of the nesting instinct. It is really rather absurd for society to be libertarian about sexual intercourse and procreation while at the same time being damnably insensitive to the necessity for homes.

37

So bad are the conditions in many urban communities, and so strong is the *sex-drive for a home* that almost any accommodation which provides shelter and sanitation is welcomed and regarded as acceptable. Thus many slum clearance schemes which provide stacked-up dwellings, like filing cabinets for human couples, come into being and are in many respects, socially and emotionally, worse than the cottage slums, back-to-backs and "bye-law housing"[1] which they replaced. Physically the flat in a tower-block may provide a better enclosed environment and much can be done with interior decoration to humanise it. For childless people who go out to work and use it mainly at night such a home may be desirable with its outlook and its anonymity, but as a family home, as modern research is increasingly making clear, it is a disaster and a cause of disaster.

A home is one's private station in relation to the rest of the community. It plays a very large part in giving one a place in society and it is linked with other homes through personal relationships. Space standards are the normal concern of people who design housing but temporal standards are just as important and these are neglected. Time comes into the problem in two ways. Firstly and most obviously in terms of communication, the time it takes to get from one place to another, from home to shops or school or work, but there is also the very important aspect of one's sense of continuity, one's relationship *backwards and forwards in time*. In an old village this can be almost overwhelming, in a modern housing estate it is a void. The sense of place, of belonging, of having roots is helped by the retention of almost any familiar feature from the past, anything which ministers to the yearning for security, and I do not mean financial and social security but that more important sense of security which comes from symbols of continuity. In major schemes of redevelopment these are foolishly swept aside. They should be cherished, but this means designing in a more detailed way than is customary or economically acceptable. Survivals are a challenge to laziness and unhappily most architects like to sweep them aside because this is the easy way.

Architects and planners tend to belong to a section of human society whose members, mainly by means of prolonged education and partly by adjustment to the necessities of their job, strike roots in their occupation. They are among the *nomads* of modern civilization and they have to accept mobility of home. But this requires a very uncommon degree of sophistication and is not without its difficulties in marital relations and in bringing up a family without roots in one place. Commonly such people spend the earlier part of their lives wandering and then "settle down". The occupational nomads, such as planners whose careers depend upon moving to obtain promotion, suppress a deep human instinct which becomes insistent at the point in their lives when they marry—the strong desire for a secure home. It is perhaps because the modern professional nomad feels that he has conquered a "weakness' in himself that he becomes indifferent to the yearnings of "ordinary people" for a way of life which he has discarded—at least for the time being.

The sophisticated nomadism of the professional is one reason why he becomes insensitive to the needs of the great majority of people; but there is also the intellectual component in his training which tends to make him rationalise and even lament that men are "non-rational entities".[2] The crux of this problem is that rationality is no substitute for wisdom. It is far too limited a tool, like a welding torch or a laser beam, extremely powerful in a limited application. As an "intellectual" he tends to value a mystical concept called "culture" which involves a great deal of talking about life and art—*prattle-culture*—rather than actually doing things, so that again he becomes separated from the people whose preoccupation is mainly with making-and-doing rather than thinking-and-talking. For the practical people who, after all, are the executants of all architecture and planning, leisure activities involve making and doing and these "hobbies" require space. It may seem to the intellectual who balances his life as an administrator with gardening or carpentry that his is a normal attitude but in fact people tend to be consistent rather than split, using their leisure time practising for themselves (and to ideal rather than commercial standards) the skills by which they earn a living.

But perhaps the greatest snare for the architect and planner lies in the fact that he has been taught to regard the practice of his art or skill as a fulfilment of himself, and it is all too tempting to see people as an obstacle to the realisation of schemes which are the projection of his cultivated powers of intuition and reasoning. It is terribly easy to become convinced that what you want to do is in the interests of humanity, and all you have to do is impose your ideas in the face of a resistance which springs from ignorance and stupidity. This disease of self-righteousness is bad enough in creative people, who at least have something to offer, but it is also endemic in administrators who seek self-fulfilment simply in the imposition of their will upon other people, often by identifying themselves with particular schemes generated by designers or with policies promoted by political and/or business interests.[3]

The whole of this mistaken and disastrous attitude is focused in the use of the word *housing* instead of *house*. It is, of course, easy to argue that with vast modern industrial populations we are *compelled* to think in terms of housing rather than houses, but this is an indication that the problem has got out of hand; it is the policy of despair if we can no longer provide adequate *homes* for people and can only think in terms of *accommodation*. It becomes tragically comic when architects see housing complexes as opportunities for the abstract composition of architectural volumes and spatial relationships. They have been conditioned in their schools of architecture to believe that this is what architecture is about and the slabs and towers of high-rise housing are far more suitable for the application, on a large scale, of the techniques of the basic art course than cottages on the ground. Within these "megastructures", as they are called by those architects who are leading the flight from humanity, the social conscience is satisfied by providing ergonomically and anthropometrically designed appliances within walls which enclose adequate space for so-called living according to a simplistic pattern of eating, sleeping, copulating, procreating, and going to work. Arguably some of the "functions of the home" can be rationalised on a co-operative basis (day nurseries etc.): very rarely indeed do such facilities begin to measure up to the need, and this may perhaps be because they are not believed in as a satisfactory substitute for the adequate home. Intellectuals tend to extrapolate from experience in middle class areas and sometimes to argue that the people who live in "housing schemes", the "working classes", are incapable of achieving a comparable degree of socially beneficial organisation. The roots of the trouble seem to lie not in people, but in the mess which has resulted from industrial exploitation. It is unwise to deny the capacity of people to create satisfactory communal life while excluding consideration of the conditions in which they are compelled to live.

Man is a social animal and has managed to survive through some hundreds of centuries largely by virtue of his ability— shared with some other animals—to form communities. Admittedly these communities were sometimes competitive and it is possible to argue that they are the basis of war. Evil though war may be it is silly to be blinded by it to all the advantages of communal existence and to the fact that man cannot survive except by communal life. No one who has studied human history in any depth can be unaware of the manifold malpractices of men, but in spite of what is most succinctly described in the word *sin* human communities have survived, and progressed in some respects. Even under the most appalling conditions, such as those following natural disasters, earthquakes, plagues and atomic bombs, men have proved their capacity for combined effort. This is true of all races and peoples in all times and it is false to argue that the people who live in slums are so sub-human as to be unable to live as human beings.

But disasters have to be recognised for what they are and it is not the people who are wrong when they are smitten by a plague. If the people of London had known in 1664 that plague was spread by fleas from rats they might have been able to avert the plague of 1665, which killed 60,000 people; but they lacked the necessary knowledge which eventually came by careful and acute observation of the facts. We also are suffering from a disease the cause of which we do not recognise. Like rats and fleas slum conditions of *over-crowding* have existed for a long time but industrialisation and the expansion of population have enormously increased the danger. It has reached disaster proportions and the scale and organisation of our society are such that the people within the areas of congestion are no more capable of collective action than were the flea-ridden inhabitants of London in 1665.

It has become a problem of government. Politicians, however, have a vested interest in short-term solutions, in answers which give them credit for tackling the problems though they are only palliatives which mask the symptoms and may exacerbate the disease. Reverting to our thoughts in Chapter 2, it is wrong to blame architects for designing high-rise, high-density monstrosities. The blame for this should rest upon the shallow thinking of sociologists and politicians, and indeed of the whole of society; but insofar as architects have actually *advocated* this kind of housing they obviously have revealed themselves as mirrors of society, not as leaders. Some of the great names in modern architecture look somewhat tarnished in this light.

The evil of over-crowding began to become acute with industrialisation. But with industrialisation ideas of social reform also developed and possibilities of practical fulfilment were enhanced by enormous increases in productivity. Unhappily the emphasis was upon money, not upon the *realities* of the standard of living; socialism accepted the capitalist preoccupation with the *means* of exchange rather than with the availability of *what* money could buy. A symptom of this is the enormous rise in the cost of shelter, to the great advantage, in terms of money, of those people who control the supply of this basic necessity. We have come to worship money and believe in the economic chimera that with more money, fairly shared out, we can all buy what we need. We can't. It just is not there. The food is not there for the increasing millions of people and the houses are not there because we don't give them priority: they follow in the wake of a distressed economic system. Architects, on the whole, have accommodated themselves to that system and served it. Their real failure has been in not saying, as experts in architecture, that almost everything they are asked to build falls short of what they, as architects, know is possible in building homes for people.

Deep at the root of all problems of providing homes for people is the lack of concern among architects and administrators, including town-planners, *for people as they are and as they want to be.* Inhumanity, lack of sympathy, lack of understanding, intolerance of ways of life which are different from our own— these are the worst sins of architects, even of those who are most socially concerned; indeed some of the most active "do-gooders" are the least humane, the true heirs of the biblical scribes and Pharisees.

Degraded urban communities have been forced by circumstances into a situation in which they are no longer capable of communal activity or action. Such areas of human occupation cease to be communities and tend to breed misery, neuroses and crime. They thus become the responsibility of the larger community, but the great mistake has generally been to concentrate upon physical amelioration without taking account of human relationships; to treat every individual as though he already had the plague instead of exterminating the rats; to think that because people belong to a grouping which has lost communal cohesion they are incapable of being responsible members of a community.

Thus housing is created and people are moved around without sympathy for human ties, and sometimes even with a deliberate policy of breaking down the rudiments of community life, possibly in the hope that new groupings may arise spontaneously. In fact the act of transplantation is always traumatic for people just as it is for plants. A newly transplanted plant is always in a delicate condition, as any gardening book will tell, and likewise with human beings, outside the small group of what I have called modern nomads. Redevelopment must take account of human relationships and insofar as the architect is concerned with re-housing he must think in terms of people and what they need in their new situation. Above all they need something to hold on to, to give a sense of continuity; I would advocate, for example, that if there were a familiar feature which was part of the character of the district being demolished, it should be preserved and re-erected at the new location. But more important is the retention of human links and of beneficial behaviour patterns. Worst of all is the planners' concept of social and occupational zoning whereby every area is a special sort of ghetto.

In many so-called slum areas a community life exists unrecognised by those who have and use the authority to destroy it. Where it does not exist or is in decline, it needs to be cultivated and this requires skills which are certainly not those of the architect or planner. Nevertheless the architects and planners can observe the environmental patterns which are relevant and workable. The traditional pattern is a community round a church. This still exists in many urban areas yet the church remains and the community is removed. If design is conceived as the adaptation of environment in sympathy with the people who inhabit it, then the art of environmental design, which is the proper concern of the architect, requires a much deeper understanding, in much greater detail, than is customary at present. It needs to be an understanding and sympathy for things and people as they are rather than a plan for the future. *The architect's job is to design for the present and, having faith in the future, leave the future to the people who will live in it.*

Long term aims can be the excuse for a great deal of inhumanity. The real skill comes in a continuous process of acceptable adaptation. The only reality is in the present, and the past. The future is something we believe in as an act of faith based upon past experience. The best hope of realising it is to live in the present and build for the present. Futurism is a confidence trick.

# chapter 7
# The Use of Land

One of the best ways of finding out what most people would like to do is to look at what the rich do, because one of the main constraints upon personal desires is lack of money. Some allowances must be made for ostentation, for the fact that, in a world of great economic and social inequalities, some wealthy people tend to take a pride in their privileged position and show it forth in ostentatious architecture. For such people the pattern, since the early nineteenth century, has been to give highest priority to public and national buildings which symbolise the system from which they benefit.[1] Next comes the home, sometimes on a magnificent scale with gardens and park land. Sometimes, on the great estates, the tenantry are housed in model villages designed by architects as an appendage to the great house. Farm buildings are generally simple and functional but ample. Then, when industry becomes the financial basis, a strange metamorphosis occurs. The factory is a bleak place of work and the workers, unlike the tenantry, are housed at minimal cost. Gradually the relationship between the great house and the factory becomes more tenuous and finally disappears, to be replaced by the board of directors, the limited liability company insured by law against the consequences of failure and dedicated to making a profit. This in turn is absorbed by take-over into an anonymous organisation dominated by men who have only an accountancy relationship with the activity of making things and the people who make them. They live in houses—often borrowed plumes of splendour—which are spacious and not infrequently have gardens, even in cities where the space required to grow a rosebush costs twenty times the cost of the bush.

This book is not concerned with the morality of riches nor with the distribution of wealth. We merely notice the habits of the rich because they are differentiated from other men only by their money. Being uninhibited by poverty they can indicate what the inhibited would like to have. There can be little doubt of the answer—an individual, distinct and recognisable family home.

But an even clearer indication comes from so-called middle-class behaviour with its sometimes quite disproportionate and crippling allocation of resources to the home and the acceptance of gross inconvenience and loss of time in commuting. The sophisticated urban intellectual may despise this way of life but the sacrifices made for it are a convincing testimony to the fact that many people deeply desire it. Furthermore, the great country mansion with its estate is in decline and wealthly people tend to have the best of both worlds, with a town apartment or small town house with every labour-saving device and a manor house, villa or "cottage" in the country.

When we think of housing for the great majority of people we are constrained by the belief that what they want is impossible to provide because there is not enough land. This assumption needs to be questioned. Housing, it seems, is the only kind of building which is constrained by lack of land. Roads, industry and business premises have priority over both housing and agriculture in the use of land. We accept a system of value judgements which holds something like the following priorities in the use of land: extractive industry, manufacturing industry, power, communications, military installations, business premises, education, housing, agriculture, recreation. Obviously there will be local variations, as when military installations take top priority because of the strategic value of a site such as Portland in England or Brest in France, or when minerals lie under valuable established industrial premises, but generally the pattern applies and the basis of all the related values is economic. The lowest monetary return per acre comes from recreational land—the Alps, the Andes, the Pennines,—and the highest, in real terms of productivity, from industry. There is a local distortion of the pattern in some great city centres where enormously high rents are earned with minimal productivity.[2]

It would, however, be quite wrong to suppose that this system of land-use values is imposed by wicked men upon a protesting proletariat. It is, in fact, endorsed by almost everybody because the great majority of people depend upon employment in work for their living. Unemployment is a grim spectre which, even in a welfare state, seriously reduces income and affronts personal self-respect, so it is tacitly accepted that housing must have low priority. I have suggested elsewhere[3] that our economic obsession with work will have to be questioned and then abandoned as labour-saving devices reduce the dependence of society upon work and give the opportunity for more and more people to cultivate the arts of living rather than living to work.[4] A change in attitudes to labour and leisure is coming about more quickly than most people realise and the growth of leisure—shorter working hours and higher wages—is already creating tremendous pressures and problems, not least of vandalism, violence and delinquency. This must lead to a reassessment of priorities.[5]

If we believe that economic aims are only tactics in the overall strategy of achieving the good life for as many people as possible the status of the home, as an element in that good life, needs reconsideration. There are, of course, not a few people who regard the home as a kind of prison and would like to see life institutionalised but this attitude may well be the product of bad housing conditions and the low priority we give to homes in allocating the use of land. There is also a tendency among critics of domesticity to see the home only in terms of tensions between parents and children, many of which are the result of bad architectural conditions. In the average small family the duration of the period of such tensions is quite short and its importance should not be exaggerated. The essence of a home is that the people who live there have their earthly roots in it and it is the place where they can gather a little of the necessary compost of living. It is natural that children should go away and make homes of their own, and if the healthy and natural opportunity to do so is available the links with the parental home may often be a source of happiness. In the jungle every seed that falls has to strive for survival in a pitiless environment but a civilised community is, or should be, like a garden. Our present attitudes, both to housing and to population, are creating "an unweeded garden" which threatens soon to become a wilderness.

Yet the generality of people accept the present scale of priorities, believing that industrial production, mainly of consumer goods, is the basis of wealth and looking no further than the shops for their food.

In England the whole population, of about forty-seven million, could be housed at an *overall density of twelve houses to the acre, four persons per house, on* 1,521 *square miles, that is a square of thirty-nine miles*. The area of the whole country is 50,869 square miles, so the area of such housing would be three per cent of the land surface. These figures are given merely to indicate the nature of the problem and put in into perspective: it would be silly to advocate housing everybody on twelfth-of-an-acre plots, and there are much better ways of planning homes, but even in densely-populated England one may doubt the necessity for high-rise housing to be imposed upon people who do not want it. The root of our trouble lies in the scale of priorities and the unmitigated extravagance of *industry* in the use of land. This is abetted by planners who seem to delight in spacing-out industrial establishments on trading estates with a prodigality which would be condemned were it lavished upon housing. Single-storey factories have obvious operational and economic advantages in many cases but if land economy is to be effected there is much to be said for *high-rise factories* such as were commonly built in the nineteenth century, and modern technology is fully capable of solving the problems involved.

The location of industry is also an important contributor to land-waste. Firstly, flat sites are preferred because they are cheaper to develop, though flatness often goes with high agricultural value. Secondly, industry cultivates dispersal which generates an enormous amount of traffic between factories. *The almost total lack of rationality in the location of factories in relation to necessary traffic between them contributes to the demand for bigger and better roads to carry industrial traffic.* Any industrialist who planned a single plant with the insouciance habitual in the location of factories in relation to each other would be considered insane. Governments concerned with the problem of providing work in areas of "under-employment" give official support to this lunacy.

Unnecessary loads are imposed upon the transport systems but it is right to recognise the crucial rôle which transport and communication systems play in an industrialised society. Instinctively, it seems, this necessity has been recognised from the early days of the industrial revolution which led to the establishment of the first efficient transport network since the fall of the Roman empire. The railways were pushed through with a zeal and ruthlessness only equalled, but not exceeded, by the modern cult of roads and air-routes. It is a modern article of faith that, however regrettably, environmental and housing standards must give way to speed of transit.

Under the Roman Empire it took about sixty hours, two and a half days, to get an urgent letter from Calais to Rome. Now it would take about five hours by air and twenty hours by rail assuming that, in each case, a special courier was employed. Postal service would take two or more days, little better than express mail at the time of Hadrian. For heavy goods the speed-up has been more effective but it is salutary to remind ourselves that the enormous technological efforts, and the vast expenditures of

money upon communication, have effected less improvement
than we tend to think. Moreover, the technological gains are
often frustrated by administrative delays such as customs, which
*we* seem to accept as inevitable, but they did not exist under the
Roman Empire.

Roads take an enormous amount of land and economy of
land-use seems to be totally disregarded. We assume that whatever
road-building is necessary to keep the traffic moving must be
done and *there is virtually no planning to reduce the need for roads*.
None the less it may be granted that the need for good roads is
paramount and land has to be sacrificed for trunk routes. What is
more serious is the amount of land given to roads on housing
schemes. Putting it very starkly, human beings are considered less
important than cars. Two-lane roads providing distribution for
goods, at minimum cost to business, are accepted as the rule
whereas gardens, playgrounds and places for workshops and
hobbies are the exception.

It would be merely tedious to elaborate this argument: one
has only to look at the map of almost any urban area to see how
land is wasted upon everything but houses. But we must notice
a disastrous side-effect of giving priority to roads. This is the
loss of pedestrian scale. In order to have "efficient" roads we
have to make much larger spaces between buildings than would
be necessary if we accepted some inconveniences and delays in
the delivery of goods and the circulation of vehicles. In this
context interesting comparisons can be made with some of the
old towns and cities of Italy and France where the tradesmen
learned, long ago, to effect the deliveries necessary to their
businesses, on foot if necessary.[6] Distance is a crucial factor in
the design of environment for communities and we waste a
tremendous amount of land in useless and ugly spaces between
buildings.

Whether land is scarce or plentiful, the design problem is the
same, and the same as it was in ages past, namely to produce a
socially viable built environment. From the tightly-planned
cities of the past there was access to the surrounding country.
Gardens did not have to adjoin the owner's house. One could go
out to the fields and gardens. The ruin came when the surrounding
land came to be developed along modern land-extravagant lines
and then the old centres degenerated. Within an urban area, speed
of transport is a very low priority provided that the area remains
small. It should follow that we keep urban areas small instead of
stifling them by expansion. If we must expand, and in many

cases it is essential, the controlling measure should be the pedestrian rather than the vehicle and this means that a city should be a collection of villages, not a strangling coagulation.

Whether a town is in a tight valley or on a hilltop, in a vast expanse of prairie or beset by neighbouring communities in over-developed countries, the problem is the same; the scale-setter is the pedestrian and transport must be seen as *an aid to the pedestrian*, a link between one viable social community and another, not as the dominant factor.

This way of thinking cuts across the doctrine of economy of scale which has obsessed administrators for too long and, happily, it is now coming to be recognised that inflation of size breeds inefficiency and lazy thinking which fails to understand the importance of detail. Large scale is *not* economical. For the architect detail is extremely important. We live with architecture in detail, not in overall massing. We cook in a kitchen and wash in a bathroom, sleep in a bedroom and maybe make model aeroplanes in a workshop or keep rabbits in the yard. We go out to the pub and the club and the shop, to school and clinic and playground and all this subjects us continuously to experience of the details of architecture. If the silhouettes and masses, the relationships of planes and spaces are pleasing it is a bonus to be thankful for, but beauty and efficiency of design *at the small scale* is what we most need and most intimately experience.

Yet to design homes for people, and groups of homes so that they form a visually and functionally satisfying environment for people, is difficult and requires dedication to design and care for people as they are in their infinite variety. It is asking too much of architects that they should achieve this in the interstices, the waste bits of land left between roads and factories. We cannot afford to let conventional economic considerations dictate the priorities in land-use.

We must also question conventional economics and technology. For example, we give far too little economic attention to maintenance costs and in technology we are obsessed by the mechanics of movement. Much of the travelling which businessmen do could be eliminated by a world-wide audio-visual service—a television version of the telephone. I suppose it would wreck the aircraft and motor industries as we now know them but this has to happen sooner or later. As communication systems improve mobility of people will become less necessary. The mobility of goods needs to be planned for economy of land and resources. We must not accept the current policy, which is that people have to live on the land left over from industrial development. Nor, in an electronic age, should we give undue priority to the mobility of people. Communication can now be accomplished by other means. [7]

**The Planner's Vision**
(*from the drawing by Simon Grindle*)

# chapter 8
# The Value of Land and the Planning Mentality

The higher the land-value the higher the buildings: that seems to be the present state of architectural development. The logic is that the more the developer has to pay for the site the more rentable accommodation he must be allowed to place upon it, and a curious side-effect is that the higher the building and the higher the cost, the smaller, in proportion to the rest of the investment, does the cost of the actual building become; thus it happens that the quality of finish reflects the price of the land. If the land is expensive the cost of high-quality building becomes a minor component in the calculation. We used to build the best buildings for God; now we worship money in our architecture.

According to socialist doctrine, land should not be in private ownership, and it is difficult for anyone who cares for the quality of our environment to deny that the public ownership of land would have enormous communal advantages, provided that there were adequate safeguards against bureaucracy.[1]

Politics apart, it is an elementary right of a human community to own its territory; the tribe its village, its cultivated fields, its common grazing and its hunting country. All of us who belong to nation states think of OUR country and identify ourselves with it, even to the extent of being willing to die in defence of it. Communists and capitalists are at one in this, but in the capitalist parts of the world there is growing disillusion as predatory private interests rape the common inheritance. Unfortunately socialist thinking is just as materialistic as capitalism and places the profit motive, for the community, just as high as capitalists place it for the individual. Marx, unfortunately, was a struggling middle-class emigré, an impoverished writer who was obsessed with money problems which warped his political philosophy. Many socialists have been poor and, likewise, over-concerned about money. A few, like Ruskin, have been very rich and their sincerity has been in question.[2] Socialism ought not to be about money except insofar as money is a medium of exchange which is valuable for attaining a better quality of living. Some socialists have realised that money is not important and can even be eliminated from the internal transactions of a community if it is truly a commune. The basis of any economy is goods and services, not money. Obsession with money is a prelude to the collapse of society. The only real wealth is in goods and services. Among the services I include design, which is vital to the quality of an environment.

Most of the land surface of Earth is in ownership. Most of it has no great monetary worth but a few tiny areas have immense value. Consider, for example, Hyde Park in London or Central Park in New York. Neither of these is for sale but if they were the price would be enormous. Buckingham Palace and the Louvre, the one as a royal residence and the other as a museum, are totally "uneconomic". The notorious Covent Garden redevelopment area in London pinpoints the lunacy of contemporary thinking. The Greater London Council seems to have started at the wrong end by assuming that the land had an intrinsic high value. In fact, given the powers that the Council had, the value was anything they chose to make it. For example, by restricting redevelopment to three storeys they could keep the price low; by allowing twenty storeys they could make it high. Land value is determined by what the community, through its representative government, allows to be put upon the land. Land values are not absolute; *they depend upon permitted use* and permitted use should be decided in the public interest. The creation of a healthy and beautiful environment is far more important than rateable value or profit from permitting undesirable uses.

It is nonsense to say that socially desirable things can't be done because of land values. Land values are created by the community and land-use must be decided in the public interest. Unhappily the administration of this idea presents a multiplicity of problems but the principle is sound.

In this book we are concerned with the theory of architecture, but architecture begins with a site upon which the foundations of the building must rest. This is part of the earth and land values clearly play an important part in the shaping of architecture. Gradually, even the water surface of the earth is coming under forms of ownership as fishing grounds are over-exploited and submarine sources of oil and gas are developed. Out in space one might expect to find sanity, but as one satellite after another is put into orbit the sky is being partitioned and the U.S.A. and Russia are busy establishing squatters' rights. From land values we seem to be moving to space values and no doubt venal architects will go along with this extrapolation of human madness.

Architecture on Earth, or even in space, is concerned with the creation of the best possible environment. If the potentialities of architecture are to be made real, land values must be determined by design. In principle we already accept this idea when the public weal is adjudged to override private interests. It began with canals, then the railways. Acts of Parliament deprived owners of their land to let the trains get through. Immense sums of money were behind the railways. Now it is the roads and whole cities are sacrificed to road programmes which are being rushed through before public opinion hardens against chaotic road transport and brings it under control. As with the railways the road programme involves a great deal of money. Likewise factory sites make wanton use of land; and even housing, which for economic reasons is planned in absurdly large parcels, is furthered in the public interest by drastic appropriations and infringement of private ownership. The sad thing is that the guardians of the public interest almost always think in terms of money and the cheapest solution in terms of immediate expenditure. Architects, and all environmentalists, must campaign for the best *design* use of land, not its economic exploitation.

The economic attitude is ridiculous. If we applied the arguments that generally prevail, with real consistency, we should pull down St Paul's cathedral in London because it does not make economic use of the site; the Palatine Hill in Rome would be redeveloped with multi-storey apartments; the Louvre would be replaced by supermarkets; and the Champs Elysées would be turned into a subway beneath massed office buildings. We cannot afford to let land values dominate design if we are to survive and there is no kind of justice in letting people make vast profits because they happen to own land in a particular place or have been shrewd enough to acquire it with a view to exploiting the public.

From land values it is necessary to turn briefly to the profession of town planning. In recent years its practitioners have earned a detestation without parallel in the history of the professions. The reasons are plain to see. Planning is an extreme development of bureaucratic power. In effect its decisions and policies are not open to public scrutiny because our system does not allow planning issues to become political issues in the majority of cases. In part this is an indictment of party politics which fail on all sides to give effective representation to opinions about vital

environmental issues, primarily because politicians are bogged
down in irrelevant doctrinal disputes.

Planning, as practised, is primitive and incompetent. It embodies fundamental fallacies. For instance, urban areas cannot
just be *planned* in the planning sense, they need to be *designed*.
The kind of skill that goes into designing a house needs to be
extended right through the environment of any community.
It is largely an architectural problem but it must be admitted that
architects, at present, are mostly ill-equipped and incompetent
to deal with it. Planners are not, and should not be, designers nor,
in most cases, do they have any cultivated knowledge of history
or the history of architecture. Often they have tiny minds befogged
by social prejudices and not infrequently their personal idea
of Utopia is a spec' builder's house on a suburban estate. Overall
planning is necessary but it seems to need men of infinite wisdom,
tact and integrity, not the large staffs of officious clerks we have at
present.

A distinction needs to be made between the conception and
continuous adaptation of the overall plan, on the one hand, and
the detailed, day to day administration of it on the other. The
talents required of an administrative planning officer for a city
are quite different from those required to prepare the overall
design. The flexible master plan requires a quality of mind which
is very rare and comparable, in the planning profession, to that
of the judge in the legal profession. The master planner needs a
deep understanding of many aspects of life and, in particular,
an awareness that his decisions are laying down the guide-lines
for the evolution of a society. At present we are creating abominable social problems by sheer bad planning; among the worst
mistakes is zoning, which divides people and sows the seeds of
social bitterness.

The job of a planner should be to facilitate the development of
happy communities, not to order people about.

In the implementation of planning the first necessity is strong
public belief that the conditions in which they live are important
and can be beautiful. Planners and architects share a good deal
of the blame for people's loss of faith in the possibility of this
happening in modern conditions. The root trouble is lack of
attention to detail. Instead of design we have overall plans, but
every house needs designing in relation to every other house.
We have lost the technique of adding and adapting. We are
obsessed by the bulldozer and thinking big. We have lost the art
of fitting the new into the old, of maintaining the sense of place

and continuity which is so important for people. We need to learn the art of graceful transition. And basic to this is a concern for people as individuals and for society as many individuals who are all interesting and deserving of what the designer can give them.

Planners are given astonishing executive powers over people and property. They are heavily subsidised, by public funds, to fight for their policies against appeals which depend upon altruistic private initiative and private money. Their idea of public participation is commonly exercised in telling the public why it is wrong. Big Brother knows best: this image fits the planners all too well. And yet, when we complain of the planning mentality and the abuse of power over against the individual, we ought also to reflect upon the impotence of planners over against powerful industrial interests, their subservience to often misguided local political policies, and the almost total lack of planning at a national and international level to achieve the best use of scarce resources and the most convenient and efficient location of industries and services.

Planning is indeed in its infancy and the self-satisfaction of planners in the face of the staggering problems they have hardly begun to think about is horrifying. But we are here concerned with architecture and the message which has to be proclaimed is that *planning is no substitute for design.* The planner should facilitate design and, where necessary, insist upon it. Far too often the ill-repute of planners results from bad architectural design, sometimes because the planners have made good design almost impossible, but usually because of the incompetence of architects and their lack of care for design values. Sadly it has to be said that bad design is endemic in public offices where the main incentive should be to give good service to the public, and good service ought to mean good architecture.

# chapter 9
# Fundamentals of Humane Design

Much of what has been said in this book so far is in protest against the conditions imposed upon architects, conditions which make it impossible for them to contribute to their full capacity; but we have recognised, from the beginning, that architects themselves are far from proficient in the practice of their art and are indeed bewildered. In attempting to meet difficulties on many fronts they have lost sight of the basic nature of their task and failed to create a theory of architecture which matches the conditions of the modern world. So far has this rot gone that many serious architects now maintain that a theoretical basis for modern design is impossible and inevitably invalid if it were to be constructed. This is tantamount to saying either that the architect does not know what his job is or, alternatively, that whatever it is he can't do it. Vague phrases like "the design of the total environment" can be both grandiose and meaningless when brought down to the earth of a specific problem. All too often design means a watered-down misapplication of the clichés of abstract painting and sculpture to buildings which have been devised according to ill-digested assessments of functional requirements. In such circumstances it is not easy for the architect to point to his work and provide any reasonable argument why it has any value other than that it stands up and provides some accommodation. He is reduced to saying "I have done it that way because I like it that way. It is the best I can do under the circumstances. I don't know why I like it but because I am, in my own estimation, a good architect, I expect all sensible people to realise that it is good architecture". This is puerile. It is not good enough. Architects seem to have lost their *raison d'être* and are rapidly losing the confidence of the public. This is a disaster, because architecture is one of the fundamental needs of mankind. The public is losing confidence: it is offered neither architecture which it can spontaneously enjoy and admire within the limited concepts and common assumptions which it has inherited from the past, nor convincing new reasons why it

*Above*: A proliferation of dull modernistic buildings. The triumph of a style over common sense because the excessive windows create abominable internal conditions in a hot climate (Marseilles). Photo, Ursula Clark

*Below*: A May midmorning and not a soul in sight! Fierce mannerism of the modern leans heavily upon the survivals of a more humane design (London, Barbican)

*Above*: The medieval organic community. Town and church have grown together (Saintes). Photo, Ursula Clark

*Below*: The legacy of *Futurismo*, Fascist architecture of an "ordered" society (Bari)

*Above*: A sense of no-place. This was designed by qualified people (Newcastle upon Tyne)

*Below*: A sense of place. A small Scottish woollen manufacturing town with character. We must recover this quality of style, appropriateness and allusion which gives a feeling of continuity and makes places recognisable (Galashiels)

*Above*: The pathetic anonymity of post-war Rotterdam slightly relieved by the survival of old lamps and the sculptured lion

*Below*: The product of harmonious evolution, care and a sense of responsibility (Ghent). Photo, Ursula Clark

Contempt for people? Abattoir (*above*) and old people's homes (*below*). The same restless, perverted architecture

*Below*: Towers with a hundred eyes: all sense of privacy deliberately destroyed. Is this the architecture of "Big Brother"?

*Above*: Old people's cottages—an attempt to create an ideal sympathetic environment (Wylam)

*Left*: The high-rise slab —perhaps the worst kind of housing for human families ever devised by man (Newcastle upon Tyne)

es, bungalow
! An extreme
ttract industry
a civilization,
f economic and
woo industry to
o, Aerofilms

The right
ground. (A
and handli
economical

Edinburgh, historic capital of Scotland as it is and, *below*, as it would be if a few more "bold architectural statements" were built

*Above*: Versailles, prototype of the big, bold statement, the mega-structure which is meant to make people feel small

*Below*: the big statement becomes ludicrous and environmentally damaging (Galashiels)

Two basic concepts in architecture, the monument and the home, the trilithon and the aedicule. (*Above*: Stonehenge; *below*: Caserta)

*Left*: The elaborated trilithonic form incorporating an arch which remains subsidiary. (Benevento)

*Right*: The aedicular form developed as the entrance to the *"house* of God". (Ancona)

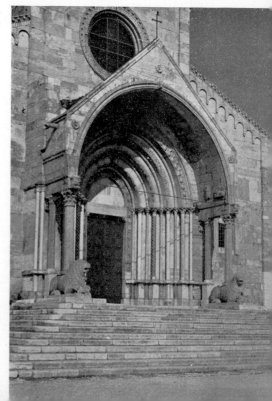

*Left*: Housing treated as an opportunity to design a monument. (Dunston)

*Below*: Architecture out of character. The strange yearning of architects to make their mark. (Princes Street, Edinburgh)

It is often said that Gothic architects always built in the "modern" style of their day. This is not true. There are many examples of their sensitive use of "period" styles to maintain over-all harmony as at Beverley, where the 13th-century triforium of the chancel is carried through into the 14th-century nave

*Above*: Rigidity of layout and ideas; the tyranny of the right-angle. Photo, Aerofilms

*Below*: The destruction of a way of life. It is astonishing with what savagery planners and architects are trying to obliterate working-class cultural and social patterns. Is it because so many of them are first-generation middle-class technosnobs?

Dead-end decoration: the ultimate banality of abstract art.

should like what is now on offer. The only convincing reasons would lie in a coherent theory of architecture, but this is lacking. Most modern architecture simply seems to be inhumane, depressing, sometimes irrational and occasionally repellent. A distinguished modern architect recently described one of his own buildings as "looking like two badly parked buses".[1] The modern movement has so far failed to come out of its period of catharsis, of rejecting the errors of the past, and to establish a modern architecture which matches the value of architecture in the past. The rest of this book will be concerned with attempting to provide a theoretical basis for the development of architecture as an art, as a humane activity whose products can be *rationally admired and emotionally enjoyed*.

We must begin with people: men, women and children, mankind at all ages from the carrycot to the grave. The average lifespan is around seventy years and the average man is middle-aged. In terms of workaday efficiency he is probably in his prime at around forty and few men go on to achieve distinction. It would obviously be foolish for the architect to design only for the children. It would be a little more reasonable to design for the elderly because they have long experience of life and possibly some degree of wisdom, knowing that they cannot live for so very much longer. It would be reasonable to design for an élite, since they may conceivably be the best judges but such élitism is hardly likely to endear architects to the majority of their potential clients. For better or worse the target for architecture is the average man and woman. Coupled, they are the typical client. They are aged about thirty-five and have children growing up. The are on the edge of the period of maximum tensions in family life and are looking forward to a period when income will be higher and commitments fewer as the children become self-supporting. By the time they are forty-five to fifty they can expect twenty to twenty-five years which, with luck, may be the happiest of their lives. This depends upon good health to some extent, but primarily upon what they have been able to make of themselves during the formative years of childhood, youth and early adult experience. Man is a slow-maturing creature with a long-life-span. This, and his extraordinary adaptability, are among the main reasons for his survival despite his obvious physical vulnerability as compared with such creatures as crocodiles.

Long-lived and adaptable. The target of the architect is not an age group or a generation but a creature called man which habitually spans three or four generations with his lifetime. His

c

adaptability in modern conditions makes him prone to exploitation. He can even make a decent life in a high-rise housing block
or a slum sandwiched between a chemical plant and a polluted
river. Human cheerfulness is no excuse for bad architecture but
the ability to be cheerful and adapt should alert us to the dangers
of puritanical ergonomics. "What a piece of work is man! How
admirable . . .". The first principle of architecture is to care about,
to be interested in, and to try to understand man, and then to
employ one's talents as an architect to serve man—whether it be
in building him a home, his first requirement, designing his place
of work, his school, his club, clinic, community centre or church.
To take the last as an example, it is not the architect's duty to
prescribe or to criticise a man's religion, but it is his job to design
the building for the practice of it. If, because of his own religion
or lack of it, he has conscientious scruples or feels inadequate or
hostile, he may decline the commission; but intolerance is no
part of the architect's commitment any more than it is part of
the surgeon's commitment to operate only on people with whom
he agrees, or the Catholic barrister's commitment to defend only
Roman Catholic criminals. The architect's job is to design buildings for people to use in the way they want to use them for the
purposes they believe in, not to tell people how they ought to
think and believe, still less how they ought to live.

For the architectural student this idea of the average man as his
notional client presents great difficulty and a challenge to empa-
thise, to feel himself into the needs and desires of the generation
from which he is conscious of growing away. But the alternative,
to design for himself as he will be when he is forty, is impossible.
For this reason the design of houses is the most difficult problem
a student can be set, and the most demanding exercise in that
talent which it is most important he should develop: his power of
empathy, of getting outside himself into the nature of his
client.

To the intellectual and the aesthete the idea of designing for
the average man may be repugnant and even shocking, but
because architecture is a public art, and every work of architecture contributes to the quality of the environment of people,
there is very little choice between designing for people as they are
and opting out of architecture in order to devote one's life to
making people better so that the standard of architecture can rise.
This was the dilemma faced by William Morris, who turned away
from designing beautiful things which only the rich could afford
in order to raise the standard of living and education of the

poor. An architect must design for society as it is and people as they are. This is the simple reason why architecture has been rightly called a mirror of society. To design beyond and above the level of public taste an architect must seek his clients among a minority, as Le Corbusier did when he deliberately chose to design for "the chosen few".[2] On social grounds many modern architects may recoil from this and on practical financial grounds they may lack the courage to design only for a select clientele, but the choice is clear: designing unpopular architecture is an élitist activity.

In the cant phrase of the moment architecture is concerned with "the total environment". If it means anything, it is the environment of ordinary average people in which it is important that ordinary average people should be comfortable.

By being an architect a man or woman does not cease to be an average, typical person. Nearly all people have some degree of specialisation in the contribution they can make to communal life; the architect simply has skill in designing buildings rather than, for example, skill in driving a train, training race-horses, ploughing a field or servicing an aircraft. He is normally an ordinary person serving a community of ordinary people which includes, if it is lucky, a few extraordinary people—men and women of outstanding quality. It is doubtful if as many as one in ten thousand of architects fall in to this genius class. The great majority are average people with a skill which is socially valuable and their rôle is to serve society by the exercise of that skill to the best of their ability. They also form the link between the rest of society, which has no special knowledge or cultivated understanding of architecture, and the few men and women of genius who are capable of contributing to the evolution of architecture. If the judgement of the ordinary architects is faulty the trend may be retrograde, so there is a high responsibility upon them to be *aware*.[3]

Behind the word *ordinary* is the fact that all people are unique and different. This the sensible architect knows from his own experience of his professional colleagues who are all, or nearly all, different from himself even within the field of architecture. How much greater the differences between ordinary people of different occupations. Society is made up of individuals to each of whom his own life is more or less the centre of the universe. Fundamental to architectural design is the tension between man as a member of a community, as a social animal dependent upon other members of the pack, and man as a unique individual whose instinct

is to differentiate himself. Most creatures that build nests conform to undifferentiated custom. Swallows build like other
swallows, choosing a site which demands the minimum of
originality in design, but man is self-conscious and identifies
his home with himself making it, in one way or another, unique.
Man should not despise his own nature in this matter: on the
contrary he should recognise that the most ordinary of men is
aware of his uniqueness and it is *natural* for man to want to
express his individuality in his home. This instinct conflicts with
ideas of architectural order and a compromise has to be reached.
The power to compromise is one of man's winning characteristics.
Individuality is sacrificed in the façades of Georgian Bath but,
inside, each house is unique.

But why are people prepared to sacrifice individuality behind
the façades of John Wood?[4] The answer is simply that as individuals they gain from something which is acknowledged to be
beautiful. It is a privilege. But the blank and featureless façades
of slabs of housing give no up-lift to anyone, only a sense of
shameful anonymity. This is the burden, the insult which housing
authorities impose upon their tenants. There is no compensation
in sharing the legacy of beauty and being able to say with pride,
"I live in The Royal Crescent," just bleak façades, just shameful
anonymity.

This, one may think, is what the little grey men who scraped
through their examinations and coveted a modest income impose
upon humanity in the name of architecture. But not only little
grey men; people of considerable talent with a strong sense of
public service also lend themselves to the creation of architectural
masses which deliberately suppress individuality. Housing becomes the medium for monumentality. The home is replaced by
a cell in a hive. People cease to be seen as individuals and become
a collective entity. Remember the fascist romanticism of Sant'
Elia and others who have conspired to make human ant hills.
The architect becomes the lieutenant of Big Brother.

"The big unit principle is indeed part and parcel of modern
architecture. When we design a façade we think in terms of a
large texture which will help mold and give character to an
outdoor space. Our façades are a kind of woven fabric, a 'rush
matting'. They can be beautiful or not, just as a Scottish tweed
can be handsome or poor. But our façades will always be elements of a greater, coherent composition—elements in the big
unit." So, presumably will the people. The writer of this passage,
Marcel Breuer, was one of the luminaries of the Bauhaus and we

may remember that Walter Gropius, its founder, was a deeply
humane man, that he left Germany because of his implacable
opposition to the Nazis and his hatred of anti-semitism. He was
one of the great minds, perhaps the greatest, of "the modern
movement" and the object of his teaching, like that of Patrick
Geddes, was to make good design available to ordinary people.
But environments have their effects in strange ways, and one
may trace back to the German environment of the 'thirties this
element of architectural fascism which is the poison in the
Bauhaus creed. It is well illustrated in the film of Schlemmer's
*Triadic Ballet*, which uses man as a sexless automaton—an
element, as Breuer puts it—in the texture of a tweed.

There is a basic wrongness in conceiving the human habitation
as an anonymous cell in a mass composition. This wrongness
arises from confusing domestic with monumental architecture.
The price man pays for neglecting monumental architecture is
to have his home reduced to an element in housing schemes
which are designed as if they were monuments. Architects seek
fulfilment in the wrong medium.

The organiser, the planner, the architect, the administrator
are all people who like to think big. They have a vested interest
in bigness, for the bigger the unit under their command the more
power and the more money they have. Legions of experts in
management have worked out a litany for the advantages of
large scale; the contrary arguments are seldom heard because
there is no power behind them. They come to be seen as the
arguments of little men, little men with whom one can sympathise
but who of course have to go down under the march of progress.
But in business and industry, and even in very large scale professional practices, the signs are appearing that bigger means *less*
efficient. When costs rise and profits fall something has to be
done; yet scaling down, subdivision, local autonomy, delegation,
all run counter to the interests of the people with most power.
The hierarchy is designed for expansion and aggrandisement—
it grinds on until it comes to a halt. Not infrequently it is then so
big and important in terms of employment that it has to be
subsidised or nationalised. Once it becomes bureaucratic very
little can be done short of revolution. Big becomes bigger and
small is absorbed. We have to live with a mystique of bigness
which gives effective power to fewer and fewer people. This is a
route to totalitarianism and spells out the death of personal
freedom. Big buildings are the architectural manifestation of
this ordering of society. They symbolise *bigness*, primarily, and

then the regimentation and suppression of inviduality which
bigness requires. Such buildings are not monumental; they are
merely big, in the way that large industrial installations, international airports and harbours are big.

It is necessary to distinguish clearly between size and monumentality. Monumental buildings are often quite small; some,
like Bramante's Tempietto at San Pietro in Montorio is minute
but it is a truly monumental building both in its purpose, which
is to mark the place of St. Peter's crucifixion, and in design. Le
Corbusier's chapel at Ronchamp is also small; the massive Arc
de Triomphe in Paris is no more, and one might think it less
monumental than the Trajan arches at Rome or Benevento.
True monumentality depends upon appropriate significance
architecturally interpreted and involves the immensely subtle
handling of scale. It may be partly because we have, as a society,
lost the taste for monumentality somewhere along the route of
our blinkered pragmatic search for a purely secular functionalism,
that frustrated architects take wrong opportunities to attempt
monumentality. It is fundamentally important to distinguish
between domestic and monumental architecture. The one is for
the living and the other is for the dead, or for the gods. Versailles,
the home of the Sun King, tried to be both and failed to be either.
It was an early example of the vulgarity of confusing mere size
with monumentality.

# chapter 10
# Aedicule and Trilithon

In 1752 Marc-Antoine Laugier made an important contribution to the theory of architecture by publishing his *Essai sur l'Architecture* in which he identified "the little hut" (*la petite cabane rustique*) as the essential form of classical architecture. His little hut had a pitched roof and columns. Roof and columns were the fundamental elements from which all architecture derives. Laugier's attitude to architecture was that of a scholar, not of a practitioner; it was intellectual and formalistic as befitted a Jesuit and his theories were notably well argued. He went so far in his next book as to say "It is for philosophers to carry the torch of reason in the obscurities of principles and rules. Execution is the proper rôle of the artist and philosophers should make the rules".[1] Laugier's rules were for classical design, though he was unusual for his age in admiring Gothic architecture, but his idea of the little hut also fitted into the philosophy of J. J. Rousseau and became a romantic ideal which flourished in simple architecture for the rich and led on, in turn, to the architecture of suburbia and the garden city. So universal is the idea of the little hut that it has even been seen as the basic aedicule of Gothic architecture[2] as well as the origin of classical form as Laugier propounded.

There are three basic ideas in architecture. They are:

*a.* The little hut, the *aedicule*, basic home of man or god, the house, the shrine, the temple.

*b.* The column, the organ of support, the symbol of generation but needing to be coupled to achieve its full significance as the yoked columns of the trilithon, as in Stonehenge. From the single sacred column, the menhir, the phallic cone, the pyramid, we proceed from what is essentially sculpture to the most powerful architectural symbol, the trilithon—two posts and a lintel. Surround the aedicule with trilithons and you have the classic temple, at once the monument and the home of a god.

Frontispiece of Laugier's *Essai sur l'Architecture*

    *c.* The tensile structure, the tent, the suspension bridge, always dependent, having to be held and so lacking a powerful symbolism. The architecture of the nomad.

Architecture is founded upon the aedicule and the trilithon. The arch, like the rope of a tensile structure, is unstable and became in classical architecture an immensely useful device—but by its nature never an element. It can serve the trilithon or the aedicule. When men learned to make lintels which were strong in tension the arch began to go out of use. It now seems strange and something of an affectation for an architect to design with arches. This is more than a change of fashion; it is the subconscious recognition of its non-elemental nature. We don't need arches any more. The aedicule has been assaulted by the invention of waterproof flat roofs so that home and monument have become confused, but generally a child still draws a house with a pitched roof and builds a play-house with one. Deprived of the devices of roofing-felt and asphalt this is how we would have to build houses. A device, the arch, becomes recessive when it is no longer necessary but a basic element, the aedicule, is not invalidated by roofing-felt.

The trilithon is monumental non-enclosing. The aedicule is domestic space-enclosing. Much of the trouble with modern architecture comes from confusing the domestic enclosure with the monument.

If we accept a flat-roofed aedicule, as may be appropriate in a hot dry country, we must draw it quite differently from a trilithon, thus:

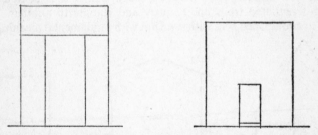

But, in fact, the aedicule in hot dry countries tends to be domed and sometimes canopied: wherever it may be the aedicule is "a roof over our heads".

In the early years of the modern movement the flat roof was one of the symbols of modernity and became something of an obsession. It was exciting because it challenged the archetype, the

C*

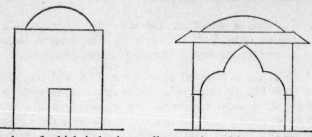

pitched roof which is basic to all countries with a considerable
rainfall. The flat roof was iconoclastic; it dethroned an image.
It also blurred a fundamental distinction. We *need* both the aedicule
and the trilithon and whatever form of aedicule we adopt we
must recognise its difference from the trilithon which has been
defined above, *domestic-space-enclosing as against monumental-
space-defining*. When the trilithon rather than the aedicule becomes
the basic element of house design man is being subordinated to
monumentality, and monumentality is, by definition, for the
dead, "something that serves to commemorate".[4] The aedicule
is for the living. The two are merged when, as in the Parthenon,
or Chartres Cathedral, the building is, at one and the same time,
the home of a living deity and a monument.

It is probably foolish to try to destroy established symbols
such as the cross, the crescent, the tricolour, the stars and stripes,
but the pitched-roof aedicule is older and more fundamental than
any of these. Essential for the recovery of humanity in architecture is acceptance of the established aedicule of the country
in which one is building. This supports the most common criticism of "modern architecture" which is that it is completely
undifferentiated from one country and climate to another. We
are not concerned here with style but with fundamental meaning.

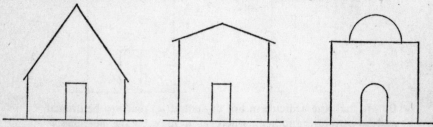

If we accept the aedicule as a basic concept of domestic design
there is an immediate challenge to the clichés of modernism and
the shapes used in basic art. The aedicule is symmetrical. The
monopitch is a rejection, a protest. It only makes sense as a

lean-to, as an adjunct and there is, of course, considerable
functional and structural justification for not using the monopitch except as a lean-to. It belongs to the *fou* period of rejection
for the sake of rejection, of the cultivation of design values over
against humanity.

The aedicule which is deeply rooted in all the cultures of the
northern hemisphere, and has been transplanted to the southern
hemisphere where in many cases it has met an identical form in
indigenous architecture, is symmetrical and has included lines
which do not fit into the traditional patterns of abstract art.
They are not acceptable because, as architectural symbols should
be, they are far too strong. Architecture is essentially strong,
stable, static, unified, complete; as such it does not lend itself to
subordination within the conventions of modern painting or
sculpture. The current need is for architects to return to their
own aesthetic, to the basic concepts of the aedicule and the
trilithon.[3]

The aedicule is age-old and fundamental, but lest this be
considered a reason for rejection it is pertinent to turn to modern
psychology and consider the aedicule in the light of gestalt
theory. Quite simply, the *gestalt*, the perceived form of a slab
or tower block of housing is the complete slab or block. This is
an assemblage, often of trilithons, to create a monstrosity.
Ideally—and here I revert to what the average man and woman
want—each home should be a *gestalt*, as it is in a village. If we
are seeking humanity in architecture we must try to make the
*gestalt* coincide with the dwelling. This is not easy, and under
some conditions it may be impossible, but it is what we should
be trying to do and our architecture should be judged by our
degree of success in achieving this.

The recovery of the aedicule involves the acceptance into design
practice of the diagonal, the isosceles triangle and the arc. It also
involves recognition of small scale as being desirable. The
aedicule and the trilithon are at extremes apart. The measure of
the domestic aedicule is man. This was dimly perceived by Le
Corbusier but in *L'Unité d'Habitation* at Marseilles he had to
make symbolic man three times life size, thus invalidating the
whole concept. (Some children had built a real aedicule, a
"Wendy house", on the waste land to the south when I was there.)
The *Unité d'Habitation* is, of course, the antithesis of the aedicule;
it is the hive over against the separate dwelling.

As Patrick Nuttgens has observed, "the dimensions necessary
for two people are more significant for planning than those

necessary for one person".[5] The aedicule is not a symbol of
personality, of individuality; it is the symbol and habitation of
the smallest communal group, the family, the pairs of human
beings and their offspring.

The relevance of the aedicule can be considered statistically.
We can take it as typical that most children remain with, or
close to, their parents' home up to the age of eighteen; if we take
the median age of marriage as being about twenty-five there is a
period of detachment from the family lasting, on average, seven
years. Thereafter marriage and the raising of a family necessitate
a family home for about twenty-five years. Most parents want to
keep a home large enough for children to visit them and generally
older people choose, if they are free to do so, to remain in the
family home until retirement. Some continue in the old home
until death; some go into smaller accommodation, but as we have
already noticed (p. 2) the ideal is then a cottage home rather than
"an institution". On this basis one seventh of the average life
span is not attached to home. Allowance for the sixteen per cent
of people who do not marry raises the average figure for the
population to about twenty-six per cent. Such figures, of course,
do not allow for an infinity of variations, such as single people
having homes, mother-and-daughter homes and unconventional
relationships.

Briefly, the relevance of the aedicule can be said to be about
seventy-four per cent. It is significant that the seven years when
it is least relevant in life coincide with the student period when
an architect is learning his job. This is the period during which,
probably more than at any other time in his life, he aspires to
design monumentally or, if he is more socially conscientious,
to solve social problems on a big scale by comprehensive redevelopment of "the total environment".

But concern for a way of living means concern for people as
individuals and as viable groups from the family upwards in
size. We are bound to think in terms of organisations but we
must never lose sight of the fact that organisations are for people,
and not the other way round. If architecture is to reflect our
attitude towards people—respect for personality, for individuality
and for the small spontaneous groupings formed out of friend-
ship and shared interests—the aedicule not the slab block, the
little hut not the cellular hive, must be one of the main bases for
our design thinking.

But society is not only a collection of individuals: by coming
together and generating organisations, by facilitating specialisa-

tion so that each individual makes a different contribution and all are dependent upon each other, a corporate existence is created. It is right to speak of *a society*, even *a civilisation*, and just as the individual or family group needs an identifiable architectural expression so the corporate body needs architectural forms which stand for it, which symbolise it and form part of the matrix of the society. By failing to recognise this polarity in architecture, this need for architecture to exist at two distinct levels, one for the individual and the small group, the other for society and the big group, we have failed in recent years to satisfy either requirement.

In ancient times, when the idea of a society was effectively expressed in a patron deity, the attributes of the monument (originally, as in the Pyramids, erected to the dead) were given to architecture, which stood for that which was enduring or eternal in the society. Thus the Parthenon symbolised Athens, its achievements and aspirations and was conceived as a shrine or home for its patroness, the goddess Athena.

The Greeks laughed at Alexander the Great when he accepted divine worship from peoples he had conquered and to them he remained a mortal man, great but not divine. This sense which the Greeks had of the dignity of the individual *as a human being* and the clear distinction man and the gods, the transgression of which was *hubris*, was an important factor in their own greatness as a civilisation—a civilisation which has probably contributed more than any other to the sum of human achievement. We do not have to believe in the gods of Olympus to recognise the value, for ourselves, of maintaining the distinction between what is mortal—the individuals of a society—and the enduring corporate ideals and images by which it exists.

In western society the Middle Ages produced a decline in monumentality, a quality which, though it persisted in Romanesque, all but disappeared in Gothic art. The trilithon was abandoned and the Gothic period made its greatest buildings, the Christian cathedrals, into *houses* of God, incomparably better in materials, structure, enrichment and the skill of the designers than the houses of men, but still houses. With the Renaissance the trilithon came back with secular symbolisms. In both religious and secular architecture a curious fusion of the domestic and the monumental occurred. It has aptly been called "The Architecture of Humanism". But Renaissance humanism, while it idealised man at the conceptual level, had scant respect for him as a person. Compassion played no part in it.

The men who made the industrial revolution turned away from man as an ideal towards the improvement of his condition by *progress*. They borrowed from the architectural apparatus of humanism but changed its character completely. They were sympathetic to Gothic revival partly because they lived in an age of resurgent Christianity, and partly because they were, though we tend to forget this fact, revolutionaries engaged in bringing about a better order of things—a mission which, with various degrees of sincerity, they believed was doing God's work. Not a few were philanthropic idealists but the continuance, into the industrial nineteenth century, of eighteenth-century agrarian standards of living for the workers produced appalling conditions which generated revolutionary movements of a different kind. None the less it was the element of philanthropic idealism which emerged as a stimulus to the pioneers of modern architecture who wanted to see both an architecture truly appropriate to an industrial civilisation and better housing and working conditions for "the workers". Gropius and Sir Titus Salt[6] had more in common than might at first appear from their architecture.

The religious element in industrial society has declined very rapidly indeed and materialism has ascended. Somewhere along the road monumental symbolism was lost. It had to go because in a materialistic society it became ridiculous. One of the last strongholds was banking, but the idea that banks stand for anything other than money is rapidly disappearing. Unhappily materialism cannot ask us to raise our eyes above the level of enlightened self-interest, and unselfishness practised out of enlightened self-interest is only selfishness by another name. If this is the best that can be expected of man monumental architecture can only be pretentious scenery: it can only stand validly for beliefs and ideals outside our individual selves. It is not, however, the purpose of this book to question the materialistic view of life (though I personally think it offers nothing but tedium and unfruitfulness for the future). The fact has to be faced that materialism leads to utilitarian architecture and if we are to consider monumental architecture as a modern possibility we shall have to proceed in the belief that there are values outside ourselves.

The starting point is the trilithon, a potent and ancient symbol, three stones erected not to provide accommodation or enclose space but to have *meaning*. It can be seen as the yoked columns significant of marriage, as the gateway of achievement through which one passes to new achievement—the triumphal arch—or as the propylaea, the portal of the sanctuary, the division between the secular and the sacred. At Euston Station in London it was the symbol of entry to a new age of communications.[7] We need symbolism and we need symbolic architecture but it is no use having symbols unless they mean something and this is, ultimately, a question of faith, a question of what we believe in. If this is so then monumental architecture in our time must wait for a new faith in values which are commonly believed in and can be expressed in architecture. Meanwhile we must maintain the distinction between the aedicule and the trilithon. There can be no monumental architecture in an age of selfish cynicism and attempts to use monumental architecture for commercial aggrandisement are merely ridiculous, like the façade of Selfridges in Oxford Street, London, or the much more monstrous monumentalisms of Hitler and Mussolini.

There have been times when the domestic and the monumental could be fused, as in Castle Howard,[8] but this was when the great house was the social and administrative centre of a region and the monument was to the institution of the Earldom of Carlisle, not to the living incumbent. Likewise Blenheim[9] was for the great general and national hero and the Dukedom of Marlborough, not for the man and woman who lived there, somewhat under protest. In palaces like Versailles or Caserta the monument overwhelms the aedicule because the royal home was the centre of the state. It would be silly to argue that the triumph of democracy and the rule of the people should mean that their homes, numbered in millions, should be treated as monuments, which is what we tend to do. Slabs of housing do not symbolise democracy; their meaning is very plain to read—it is the subjugation of the individual, the suppression of freedom. If they are a monument to anything it is to bureaucracy. But even in this they fail because they are neither aedicular nor monumental. They are merely big, and size has no architectural value. We can't compete with mountains.

# chapter 11
# The Architect and his Ego

It is current dogma that a work of art is an expression of the artist. This is believed more fervently by those who do not practise an art professionally than by those who do. It is endemic among schoolteachers who use artistic activities as an emotional release from the stresses of intellectual learning. Linked with psychological theory art comes to be seen as a safety valve and as a means of cultivating and expressing the self. Thus it comes about that many young people embark upon a course in art, including architecture, not in the belief that they have a craft to learn but convinced that a technique will evolve from the continued practice of expressing their emotions. I have discussed this strange phenomenon at some length elsewhere[1] but it must be mentioned in the present context because the modern practice of architecture is confounded by the yearning of architects to express themselves in their work.

It is undoubtedly true that any arduous creative endeavour such as designing a fine building, or sailing a yacht, requires that the executant should put himself heart and soul into his work, that he should take pride in it, spend himself upon it; but this is quite different from Expressionism which, oddly enough, commands little respect when recognised for what it is. Truly the artist who would achieve greatness has to forget himself, to "die to himself"[2] and become the vehicle for the creation of something which comes from all the stimuli which actuate his work. In the case of a work of architecture, site and environment, significance, client, community, cost, structure, function and many other factors are focused in the mind of the architect, where the design is created through a process of challenge and response between the mind and what is externalised as the evolving design on the drawing board. The architect is the medium, but he is capable of intervening and imposing his will as one of the stimuli, even as the main stimulus.

Behind this lies the little-understood phenomenon of artistic originality. It is a peculiarity of our time, fostered by art critics,

72

that originality is greatly admired. Ambitious architects have
yearnings to be original which resemble the yearnings of some
religious people for martyrdom; there is the same element of
insincerity in both. Originality cannot be sought or commanded:
it happens or it does not and there is nothing we can do about it.
Being *different* in order to appear original is merely fraudulent.
There have been very few notably original minds in all history
and of these few a tiny fraction have been architects. It is therefore
reasonable for any architect to inspect original tendencies in his
work with some scepticism. If there is real originality in any
degree the best thing is to forget about it, strive for quality and
give the tender plant of originality a chance to grow and blos-
som on its own.

Most design is rearrangement within the current idiom, yet
work can be dull or fresh. Dull design seems to come from design-
dull people, just as some people are natural conversational bores.
By and large I suppose they are insensitive people. Freshness comes
from a lively awareness and response to all the stimuli of the
programme. Again the design-character of the architect comes
through, but it is not deliberate self-expression nor is it originality
of the kind that Bach brought to music or Michelangelo to
sculpture. There is a touch of originality in fresh design in that
it is a fresh response, within the idiom, to a unique programme,
and it is by this kind of aliveness to the stimuli that architectural
style slowly evolves. Originality goes further and of itself creates
new stimuli in the minds of architects.

As a student, and later in practice, an architect acquires a
vocabulary just as a child learns to talk, then to write. At present
the vocabulary is meagre because in the modern movement we
started a new language, and it is not like learning afresh some old
language with a big vocabulary to discover as we progress. We
are making a new language as we go along. Any such terminology
is confined to the thoughts and experiences we have had. We do
not have "words" for things we have never seen or envisaged.

Along with this meagre language we acquired austere architectural puritanism: the modern movement has somewhat re-
sembled England under Cromwell or Geneva under Calvin.
There are those who crave for a "restoration", a return to classicism or eclecticism,[3] but this is not a way forward. What we need
is to build on the foundations of the modern movement, ampli-
fying its austerity by admitting, firstly, that human beings are
more important than doctrine and secondly by opening our
minds to enjoyable modes of architectural experience. The latter

is to be accomplished not by enacting a charade from the past, but by adding new words to our new language, new words in our architectural vocabulary which express architectural values which we have hitherto excluded from our way of designing.

Architecture is a phenomenon of all human civilisations and its values are timeless. We should look back into history, not to see how to do things but to see what things architecture *can* do which we have lost the habit of doing; and we should look at the stimuli of the present, and above all the needs of modern man, to see what else needs to be achieved. We need not seek originality in ourselves when such enormous challenges exist in the provision of a civilized environment for modern man, equipped as he is with resources that have never before existed. The question is how to use them and this is a question which requires design solutions from architects.

If we take a *total view of architecture* with its timeless values, we may discern certain recurrent patterns of change. History never repeats itself exactly but our present condition is not as unusual as we are tempted to think. Although it can be misleading to study architectural history, or the history of any art, without relating it to social history, in the total view there seem to be tides of change which are autogenous to architecture. The intellectual discipline of the Parthenon gave way within twenty years to the deliberately perverse asymmetry of the Erechtheum; the austerity of Early English Gothic gave way suddenly, at the beginning of the thirteenth century, to the exuberant naturalism of the so-called Decorated style. In Italy, the High Renaissance based upon Alberti's theoretical discipline suddenly gave way to Mannerism in which architects like Giulio Romano, trained in the discipline of classicism, broke the rules "for kicks". And again at the end of nineteenth-century eclecticism, and the futile battle of the styles, Art Nouveau rejected style to create an anti-style. The pace has quickened and the modern movement, little more than half a century later, has run its cathartic course; a new mannerist architecture, anti-functional and anti-rational is already with us. If the cyclic pattern is any guide the Erechtheum led to Hellenistic sensuousness in architecture and the popular appeal which the Romans endorsed for half a millenium. Decorated led to Perpendicular in England, an austere style which flourished after the Black Death in a period of labour shortage and rising costs, but in France Gothic developed such structural fantasies as Rouen cathedral and St Maclou. Bramante led to Giulio Romano and then to the splendour of the Baroque. Art

Nouveau was followed by pompous decorated classicism. What next?

The current interest in Mannerism and Art Nouveau is symptomatic and self-expression is sought in manneristanti-functionalism. This is anti-architecture, instinctive protest against functionalism, the worship of technology, the cult of cost-effectiveness and even the social utility of architecture. It can only be an interlude and its products will take their place among the oddities of history.

Mannerism takes no account of people. It is individualistic, selfish and quirky, not a theory of art but an anti-theory, yet it is always dependent upon knowing the rules it is breaking.

There have been many theories of architecture, most of them concerned with geometry and formal relationships, but some have been concerned with the social significance of architecture. Ruskin, for example, expounded a kind of spiritual functionalism: "Architecture is the art which so disposes and adorns the edifices raised by man, for whatsoever uses, that the sight of them may contribute to his mental health, power and pleasure."

The idea of eclecticism, of making a synthesis of all that was best in the architectures of the past, was not unreasonable and appealed as a theoretical basis, especially in Britain, at a time when colonies were being acquired like picking applies in an orchard and the British Empire was seen as the largest imperial synthesis since the fall of Rome. Probably all theories of architecture which have gained wide acceptance and been related to good architecture are of some value but, though all have elements of truth, none is complete and no theory of architecture can, of itself, mould architecture if the time is not ripe for it. Architects do not live and design by theory—but they are prone to accept a theoretical basis which is in tune with the time. The theoretical basis provides a means of talking and thinking and criticizing. It can enable one to believe that what is really a change of fashion is a fundamental invention or rediscovery of architecture. We should not despise theory; but if we can take a total view of architecture we can see that a contemporary theory-based fashion of design is not immutable truth for all time.

The great majority of architects do not design from theories or first principles. They work within a current idiom and imitate each other, thus creating the recognisable style of their period. So convinced do some designers become that the current idiom is "right" that they become moralistic about it and make it a matter of personal artistic integrity to design within the style. The danger of this moral attitude is that it is self-centred (like a great deal of other so-called morality) and the designer's idea of himself, his artistic morality and the expression of himself in his work lead him to impose his particular morality upon other people—his clients and those who are going to live in or use his buildings. The comparative study of architectural theories is a useful antidote to this unpleasant and disreputable form of architectural priggishness.

Modern architects, that is architects who think of themselves as practising within the modern movement, commonly regard this movement as being the only true architecture of our time and for the future. Generally they do not recognise that it rests upon a theoretical basis which contains some strange assumptions and some even stranger omissions and ignorances. Cocooned within the movement (which in fact has now become stationary), they have no total view of architecture and are often completely ignorant of all other kinds of architectural style. The comparison with seventeenth-century religious puritanism is strikingly valid. With people who are absolutely certain that they are morally right no argument is possible. Yet everywhere there is dissatisfaction with modern architecture. The movement has ended and is crumbling.

Imperfect and blinkered though it was, *we should not reject the modern movement and seek to go back to the early part of this century as some people are currently doing*. We should not escape into the snobbish sniggering of Pop Art[4] (aesthetic slumming) or the irresponsibility of Mannerism. The weakness of the modern movement lay in the narrowness and bigotry which may have been necessary for its early progress. In common with much social and political thinking during the period of its growth it was pragmatic and materialistic. As we have already suggested, its aesthetic was abstract and formal, unconcerned with humanity. The social thinking was of two distinct kinds, one concerned with the practical welfare of the common man and the other (as in Futurism) with fascism and the enslavement of the common man. Functionalism can mean almost anything but in the context of the modern movement it meant that design came from the solution of practical problems, the typical example being a tool whose "beauty" derived from fitness for its purpose. Modern architecture was highly moral; its exponents have been deeply concerned for the good of people and have given people what they believed to be good for them. Like the priest in *Don Quixote* the architects have said "We know what's best for you".

What is now necessary is to humanize the modern movement.

This would mean a fundamental change from élitist big-brother-liness to sympathy with people and concern for what they want, what they will enjoy and what, in a civilised society, they have a right to expect.

Architects may remain egotistical, but self-satisfaction in their job must change from giving people what is good for them to really studying people as they are and trying to give them what they will enjoy. Unfortunately many architects, and other people, think it is menial to serve people and dignified to order them about. I think such belief is rooted in a wrong view of life, but that is outside the scope of this book.

# chapter 12
# The Quality of Home

Architecture begins at home. The most fundamental duties of a
human community are to ensure that its members are fed, clothed,
housed and protected from predators. This is the primitive basis
upon which civilisation may grow and without which it cannot
reasonably be expected to survive. We pay a great deal of attention to security but are learning that the old military means are
no longer effective and have become suicidal. Food and clothing
are the basic economic concerns of every government; in crowded
modern societies we accept a great deal of housing—much of it
modern—which is sub-primitive. Standards which would be
acceptable in a primitive village are debased to intolerable
squalor merely by increase in numbers and area. A small community can manage with cess pits but a bigger one must have a
sewage system. It is the same with most of the factors which
make up the human environment. At the beginning of the
industrial revolution dreadful conditions were created by building
towns to traditional rural standards. Gradual amelioration has
not altered the original mistake of failing to recognise that in
modern, large, industrial societies the provision of homes is a new
kind of problem demanding fresh thinking in architectural design.
A start was made with pioneer developments such as Saltaire,
then later New Earswick and Port Sunlight, but these were
related to a single industry and the great slum-clearance schemes
of the last thirty years have, to a lamentable extent, replaced one
kind of slum by another. If society is to be healthy there must be
decent homes: this means a re-scaling of land-use priorities
before the architects can begin to operate satisfactorily. It is
therefore essential that architects should state, and make clear to
all concerned, the base-line from which they can start. Otherwise
they will have to bear the blame for unsatisfactory buildings
which never could have been satisfactory because the primary
conditions of fulfilling their purpose did not exist.

At this point I must recall the warning in Chapter 3 that an
architect is not a politician. It is not his job to make the right

conditions in which to design but it is his absolute duty to define and stand up for the conditions without which it is impossible for him to do his job properly. It is in this respect that architects have most signally failed to carry old standards of design integrity into the twentieth century. It has been a failure at the professional level more than an artistic failure. The artistic disaster is consequential to the miserable professional performance. The primary obligation of professional integrity is not to debase standards of design. It is far more serious to cut design standards to get a job than it is to undercut fees. This is where the architectural profession, especially in Britain, has gone off the rails.

This is highly relevant to the problem of designing homes for people. It is the architect's job to find out what his clients require, use his expert knowledge to help them in formulating a programme and then design what they need and will like within the budget available. With the exception of a very small number of privately commissioned, mostly rather expensive houses, neither the site nor the budget is under the control of the client or the architect. The true client is not the speculative builder or the housing authority but the person who is going to live in the house. He may not be a particular person, and the house will change occupancy from time to time: the real client is a succession of people who are going to live in what the architect designs. To the speculative builder houses are an industrial product which he produces as cheaply as possible to sell at a profit; to the housing authority they are a statutory duty. The speculator and the authority should be seen as agents beyond whom there are real people with whom the architect is truly concerned.

In countries with expanding economies, rising wages and growing population the people are open to gross exploitation by speculators and housing authorities because they are glad to accept almost any accommodation. The speculators can sell as fast as they can build and the housing authorites, with their persistent nineteenth-century attitudes, fulfil their obligations at the minimum cost and with negligible expenditure of imagination and design care. It is symptomatic that whereas private clients expect to pay an architect more than the standard fee for designing a house, the profession recognises that the fee for "housing" is on a reduced scale.

The basic requirement for a house in a civilized community is that it should be so sited and designed as to facilitate a way of life consonant with the level of civilisation which that society has achieved. Most housing is below the level for which modern people have been educated and which could be economically sustained if we had our priorities right. A great deal of thought, research and design need to be given by architects to establishing what modern people need and would like to have. To hell with standards based upon nineteenth-century attitudes to housing the workers, and a curse upon socialists who think good design is only for the rich.

A home is, by its nature as a human habitation, small. If it reaches the scale of a great-house or palace it has become more than a home, but even palaces have tended to preserve a domestic significance by the use of aedicular features. Even medieval cathedrals, which are aedicular, though conceived as the house of God, are not large in scale. The evidence of architecture could suggest that, with the Renaissance, Christians lost the sense of intimacy with God.

In domestic architecture intimacy is a desired quality because it is relative—it relates individuals to one another while preserving their individuality. Within a house family relationships provide the intimacy and personal privacy becomes a value; but in the relationship of houses in a community the quality of intimacy is generally desirable though some people prefer seclusion. Many medieval towns achieved both a sense of intimacy and private seclusion. This ought to be possible in modern terms. The opposite is exemplified in modern slab and tower blocks which suppress the individuality which is a prerequisite of intimate relationship, and offer only the specious seclusion of anonymity which is the condition specially dear to villains. For most ordinary people it is almost a synonym for loneliness.

The natural level of communication is the ground. There is no communication between fifteenth-floor apartments though they be only a few metres apart. It should be an elementary right of human beings to live near the earth and to come together easily upon the earth's surface. If there must be tall buildings let them be offices, hotels and apartments for childless sophisticates, if they wish, but never homes which people are compelled to take because of shortage.

The problem of designing a house in a town almost always includes the problem of relating it to other houses. Together houses form the background of the external, communal environment. It is essential to preserve the aedicular quality, the sense of a group made up of individuals. This is a problem of scale, of preserving smallness of scale. Buildings of small scale provide an interesting challenge to the architect and afford much more opportunity for design. In the small scale building every detail counts and is noticed. Mass effects are impossible, and so they should be because we are dealing with individual people not masses.

We have become preoccupied with formal relationships, the boring clichés of the basic art class, and have lost the art of decoration. This must be recovered. We need decoration, the sensitive handling of details, the apt choice and variation of materials. If we could shed our trilithonic obsessions we should discover a new world of architecture and, looking back, we should probably make new historical assessments. Perhaps the Bauhaus was a valuable purgation but we can't live in the loo for ever.

The common objection is, of course, that we must make use of mass-produced components; but we have to consider the extent to which this is an ad-mass confidence trick. The truth of the matter is that while many components such as light switches and kitchen cabinets are better produced industrially, the fabric of low-rise buildings can be flexible in traditional materials without additional cost. Indeed the popularity of high-rise building in recent years is in large measure a feed-back from the technical innovations which have made them possible and the vested interest which industry has in exploiting these techniques and the manufacture of components. This is all a matter of money, not people. If modern techniques only achieve greater cheapness we are on a downward course. Architects should be using such economies to achieve design advantages, better materials and finishes, better workmanship, and more decoration by artist-craftsmen. It really is ludicrous that we should be conned into believing that with all the wealth and technical resources of the modern world we are the only people in all history who can't afford the pleasures of fine materials and ornament in building.

Here it is necessary to mention the problem of antiquated attitudes in the trade unions which actively discourage individuality, foster demarcations and believe that all the problems can be solved in terms of improved wages. A decent standard of living should be available to every member of a modern society and trade unions have, in the past, done a great deal to achieve this objective, but job-satisfaction and quality of living have actually been impaired and a revolution in trade union thinking is long overdue. Good architecture requires good workmanship and upon both the contracting and the labour sides of a building industry which is hopelessly divided the primary aim of "well building" is frustrated. At the domestic level good architecture requires

that builders as well as architects should believe that people
matter, that building is for people and an essential component in a
civilised way of life, not just a means of earning money. The sad
fact about trade-unionism is that it has turned labour into a
medium of exchange for money.

The onus is upon architects to say what is required for good
architecture. This is a collective professional responsibility and
if the present system does not produce satisfactory results architects should be saying so in the cause of good architecture. It
is not enough to form building teams at drawing office level.
The whole business of building, including the men who actually
do the work, is concerned with *building for people* and perhaps
the greatest weakness of modern architecture is in management
in the building industry with the corresponding antagonisms
among the workers. This is even worse than the cat and rat
relationship between the architect and contractor. Quality of
craftsmanship is necessary to aedicular architecture. This requires
respect by the craftsman for the architect and good management
in between. It is not an insoluble problem. The first essential is
that it should be stated and upheld by architects.

A home should be identifiable in a way that a storage bin is
not. A mere number on the door is not enough. The home
should have an immediate perceptible environment which
consists of its relationship to other homes and facilities. The basic
unit is still what it always was, the village, the discernible community environment and many of the most successful cities have
preserved into the twentieth century the quality of being a collection of villages. Modern planners are wantonly destroying this
enormously valuable asset and laying up a tremendous amount
of social trouble for the future. Within reach of home there should
be the facilities which the community requires. These are largely
a matter of established convention but the essence of a community
is that it should be able to grow and change within itself. It
requires internal flexibility and a high degree of autonomy if a
sense of communal responsibility is to develop.[1]

The city as such is not a social community but a service area
for a group of communities. It provides facilities such as big
stores, hospital centres, business, professional and commercial
precincts, concert halls, hotels, theatres and, traditionally, a
cathedral, all of which depend for support upon the group of
communities. It can offer to its residents a different and more
sophisticated kind of living and it is a magnet to people who cherish
what they may believe to be a more highly civilised way of life.

The "culture" of cities has greatly enriched the world; it is important that they should be preserved from peripheral urban growth which strangles them. Many cities have reached maturity and need to be preserved from destructive redevelopment. A mature city is a very precious thing.

But the vast majority of people do not live in cities and even if, nominally, they do so, as in the sprawling suburbs of London, they are not involved in it as a city: they are part of a conurbation. The quality of home life depends to a very large extent upon what is within a half-mile radius and this should touch the town centre in an urban area. Throughout, the scale should be domestic, human, intimate. Necessary big buildings should be articulated so that they do not obtrude. The values of the community should be reflected in the scale of its architecture, emphasis being given only where it is due. Thus in London it was right for St Paul's to dominate the scene, as it used to do, but the Hilton Hotel is a monstrous vulgarity. Every building is important in its environment. There are no buildings which we can afford to have badly designed.

# chapter 13
# A Theoretical Basis

In Chapter 10 we identified two distinct kinds of architecture, the domestic typified by the aedicule and the monumental typified by the trilithon. So fundamental is the distinction that, since the Renaissance, many people have thought of the first as mere building and only the second as meriting the name architecture. With this long entailed legacy of prejudice in favour of monumental trilithonic architecture the younger architects of today have often rejected what they have called "Architecture with a big A" as being meretricious and out of tune with our time. Unfortunately, in so doing they have unconsciously accepted the dogmas of neo-classicism and failed to recognise that the other side of the coin is equally to be called Architecture. We do no good by regarding aedicular building as non-architecture. It seems to me that we have reached a stage in social evolution when the aedicule, the symbol, if you like, of the common man, is more important than the trilithon. There are two kinds of architecture and the aedicular kind is now ascendant.

Underneath the stylistic superficialities of the Gothic revival there was awareness of important truth. The medieval city was aedicular, dominated by the house of God around which clustered the houses of men, often gathered in by a wall to form a tightly-integrated community. It is significant that the Renaissance began in Italy when the cities became dominant and the nobility moved in from their predatory castles to build, first, tall towers and then semi-monumental *palazzi* within the city walls. The Medici bankers established this image of a new dominance in cities based upon usury, which had been anathema to the medieval way of life. Classical architecture since the Renaissance can be seen as the outward symbol of devotion to the god of money and even the modest façades of Bath or Bedford Square in London stand for respectability based upon bank balances. It is purse-proud architecture, but like all great art it is outward-looking, dedicated. The object of dedication is a way of life, the bourgeois virtue of respectability based upon prosperity.

The dichotomy of architecture was accentuated by the conditions of the industrial revolution and the population explosion which accompanied it. So much building was required in the first half of the nineteenth century in the developing European countries, and especially Britain, that the architectural profession could not expand rapidly enough to cope with more than a small fraction of it. Thus immense opportunities came the way of the few good architects in practice. From Inigo Jones at Covent Garden, to the Woods at Bath and the Adams in London and Edinburgh, leading architects had designed ordinary houses; but in the nineteenth century "housing" passed to illiterate builders. It would be unfair to blame such men as Cockerell, Smirke, and Barry for accepting the marvellous commissions that came to them instead of building rows of houses and cottages. But a pattern was established and still persists, a pattern wherein the most talented architects still covet "trilithonic" opportunities and fail to recognise the great change which is coming about—fail, in fact, to move into the modern world but instead try to impose the concepts of monumentalism upon homes and living cities.

If monumental architecture is required (and in my view there are conditions in which it still is necessary) the principles have been well worked out and I shall not reiterate them here.[1] What we need is a theoretical basis for aedicular architecture.

Fundamental is the Earth, the small planet upon which we live and which needs our care. Architecture is an adaptation of the earth's surface made with materials taken from the earth. The building of anything is a responsibility. It must be undertaken within the concept of cultivating the earth and the purpose is to alter a part of the earth in order to create a modified environment for the benefit of man.

Man is a creature of Earth, born of it and returning to it. His place is upon its surface and his life depends upon air and sunlight. Architecture is a kind of cultivation. Cultivation seeks to conserve and improve; it must not damage. If we see Earth as a quarry, to be exploited to exhaustion, we have no faith in man or the future of man. If we see it as a garden it can be adapted and improved, growing under our care.[2]

Human needs are physical, emotional and intellectual.[3] Physical needs are catered for by functionalism, by designing the building and all its parts so that they work as well as possible; but inevitably there are conflicting functions so every building must embody functional compromises based upon the judgement of the architect. The cultivation of this faculty of wise judgement is one of the principal aims of architectural education. It must depend equally upon understanding of buildings and of people. At the functional level it is the job of the architect to make the buildings fit the people. People are not static entities: they grow and change throughout their lives and most buildings are for more than one person. Relationships change. It is a functional necessity to provide flexibility. Once the architect has finished, if not before, the occupier takes a hand in the design by adapting the building to his changing needs. Adaptability is a functional necessity. It is part of the design problem and there must be limits. The extent of these limits is one of the compromises which require design judgement by the architect. The greatest danger is the élitist trap, that the architect knows best what is good for the occupier—"Big Brother"—when in fact the architect is only impressing himself and his cronies.

Emotional needs are of many kinds and far too little study has so far been made by psychologists of the relationship between people and buildings. Peoples' feelings about buildings cover a very wide range but the most basic is the sense of *home*. About this it is easy to be facetious and shallow simply because the feeling is so deep. Even the most inveterate wanderer and the most detached cosmopolitan has some place where he feels he has roots, some place from which he sprung or, failing that, some place from which his people came. There may be advantages in suppressing the sense of home, in achieving a kind of independence or entering a monastery, but for the vast majority of people for whom an architect designs, the place at which a man is plugged into Earth is important to him. The comparison with a power socket is not unreasonable: it is the point at which he is earthed.

On an earth inhabited by some four thousand million people it is difficult for the individual himself to believe he matters. It is not easy to answer for sure the questions Who am I? What am I? Basic to a sense of security is the possibility of saying "I am the man who lives at . . .". Location is one of the conditions of self-awareness and self-confidence.

"*I know where I'm going, and I know who's going with me.*" That is quite a proud statement. More modest and more basic is *I know who I am and where I live*. One does not need to wallow in the sentimentality of *Home Sweet Home* to recognise that a sense of place, a sense of *belonging* to a place, is helpful to people. It is more important to belong to a place than to own it and it seems to me that, in the modern world, the private ownership

of land is out of date and as irreverant as private ownership
of a church. We are incumbents, tenants, not owners of parts of
Earth; a great many of the problems of modern architecture
would be at least partly solved if this principle were accepted.
To say that one owns a part of one's mother, Earth, is an impiety.
To make a profit out of selling parcels of her is monstrous.

The intellectual needs of man are not peculiar to "intellectuals".
Most people, and certainly all who are entitled to be considered
educated, like to and indeed must think about their environment.
At its simplest this means it must make sense; at what can be
considered higher levels it may be the intellectual component
in aesthetic experience; but at whatever level the architect and
planner try to operate they must expect to be questioned. If his
work does not make sense to the ordinary man the onus is upon
the architect to explain. Furthermore the architect must pre-
consider the acceptability of his justification or explanation.
For example, in some cases humour may be appropriate and
without actually explaining the joke an architect may indicate
his intention and ask people to smile with him. But if he makes fun
of a crematorium he is giving offence. His joke is out of place.

The intellectual, the aesthetic and the emotional are closely
linked but it is well to recognise that there is almost always an
intellectual component in any work of art. In a great work of art
the aesthetic value can be appreciated at various emotional and
intellectual levels. The Parthenon, Chartres Cathedral and the
chapel of Nôtre Dame at Ronchamp can all be appreciated by
very simple people, as Tolstoy said they should, but the astonishing fact about great works of art is that this simplicity of appeal
comes *not* from playing to the gallery but by creating works
which are *also* accessible at high levels of intellect and emotion.
The simplicity is deceptive. Hence arises a dreadful misunderstanding whereby artists, including architects, consider it meri-
torious to make works which are only accessible to an élite. The
secret of really great work is that it achieves simplicity by ap-
proaching perfection so that the more it is studied the more is
found in it. The simple and sincere mind apprehends the quality
that is there without fully understanding. But the quality has to
be there. Perfection is complete simplicity, which is the hardest
thing of all to achieve.

There is no virtue in being complicated, obscure, inaccessible
and tortuous in order to appear to be interesting and original.
That is just monkey-puzzle architecture.

Architects have no absolute right to continue practising in the way they fancy and according to whatever architectural or other principles they favour. The establishment of national institutes, even under royal patronage, as in Britain, lays no obligation upon people to employ a kind of architect which has become irrelevant. Architecture is total and coterminous with civilisation but architects are not, and if architects of the establishment fail to provide what is necessary a new kind of architect will come into being. In Britain, because of the Architects Registration Act, the name "architect" would be restricted for a time to people who, in a modern context, were not acceptable as architects until legislation caught up with actuality—which might take a quarter of a century or more. The outstanding example of the displacement of one kind of architectural profession by another is provided by the eclipse of the medieval master-mason-architect by the Renaissance artist-architect.

I have suggested that few architects are aware of a theoretical basis for the way they design: mostly they imitate, but in any way of design there is a theoretical basis, whether it be implicit or explicit. In High Renaissance architecture theory was fairly explicit; in medieval and modern architecture it was and is mainly implicit. There is no accepted formulation of the theory of modern architecture but there are basic assumptions which most modern architects seem to regard as "self-evident truths". Both the truth and the evidence need scrutiny. What seem to be eternal and self-evident truths are all too often opinions based upon value judgements which happen to be in accord with the generality of thinking at the time. When Ruskin said that "Architecture is the art which so disposes and adorns the edifices raised by man, for whatsoever uses, that the sight of them may contribute to his mental health, power and pleasure"[4] he was sincere and approved by many, probably most of his contemporaries. When Tolstoy said that all that was good in art was comprehensible by the simple peasant he was entitled to respect.[5] He was not an ignoramus nor a fool but his attitude was totally different from Le Corbusier, who said that art was for "the chosen few".

A new theoretical basis needs to be established, a theoretical basis in tune with what people are *now* thinking about the relationship of themselves as individuals to society and the environment. The basic evaluations are totally different from those which were current in the first quarter of this century when the modern movement was cast into shape.

First comes man's collective responsibility for the conservation of Earth. Man seems to have become trustee for Nature, if only because he has the technical means of destroying most of Nature and rendering Earth barren. *Keeping the peace* is man's most significant duty. Whatever way one looks at it, whether from the religious or the materialistic viewpoint, war is the greatest crime, the most dangerous evil. No cause can justify the use of war, not just because men, women and children must inevitably suffer by it but because millions of years of evolution upon Earth would be irreversibly destroyed by war with modern weapons.

The next priority concerns the balance of Nature. Science has so protected human life that disease no longer keeps population under control. War is no longer an acceptable means of population reduction. The onus is now upon man to preserve a balance between himself and the rest of Nature upon which he is dependent for most of what he values in living. It is not the architect's or even the town-planner's rôle to say how men should control population but it is essential that architects and planners should present, in coldly factual terms, the environmental implications of population explosion. Mostly sociologists and ecologists have worked on this problem but the people who are concerned with the *design* of environment must think and speak out about the design implications of over-population and indicate the limits beyond which environmental design would have to abdicate. Architects and planners must look at the viability of human communities in terms of environmental design and make their contribution to the creation of a beneficial balance of mankind in Nature. Such considerations which concern the survival, not only of man but of all species on Earth, must take priority over social justice among men, important though this may be.

Next comes social justice which, for two hundred years, has obsessed the minds of those who were underprivileged and those with privilege who cared about those who lacked it. The record of history shows that those with some privilege, and a sense of obligation, have contributed far more than the underprivileged themselves to the promotion of social justice. The reason for this is simple, that those without privilege were also largely without education or influence. The social revolution has been brought about by idealists, most of them middle-class like Voltaire, Rousseau, Lenin, Robert Owen, Karl Marx, William Morris and Walter Gropius.

Architects have nothing to boast about in the social revolution: they have generally served their paymasters. This is not a

D

reproach; it is simply an indication of the reality that architects exist by patronage, like portrait painters, museum curators, actors, novelists, supermarket directors, publishers and even doctors and lawyers who have to be on the acceptable side of the credibility gap to survive.

Social justice is only relevant to architecture when people believe in social justice. Some of the most beautiful buildings ever designed have had no social justification by socialist standards. It is only when socialists believe that architecture matters and that everybody has a right to beautiful buildings that we shall achieve a beautiful built environment. No, that is not quite true. If we really did have an élite who truly believed that God's in his heaven and all's right with the world and who wanted to ensure that even the lowest dependents lived in beautiful cottages we might have a kind of Utopia.[6] It nearly happened in the eighteenth century, but foundered on the ubiquitous rocks of greed and stupidity. The architect can only do what the society of his time allows him to do. His art is expensive and depends upon money. Who pays the piper calls the tune.

Yet the majority of people live in built environments and the remaining minority in humanised landscapes. Design, mostly bad, in everywhere between sea level and two thousand metres. Within this miniscule belt of atmosphere on a tiny planet architects operate.

Humility is the other face of social justice. If every child born onto the earth is to have a decent chance of survival and development to the levels of selfhood which we now know to be possible, the architect is not to be concerned with an élite raised to privilege by inherited or acquired wealth but with the built environment of all men, some four thousand million of them who all have the same kinds of feelings and capacity for joy and sorrow, for ecstasy and pain, for loving and for generating.

Architects and planners have a part to play in creating the environment but, again, they have to sell what they believe to be valuable to their economic masters. In the modern world architects must be concerned with environmental values and must explain what it is that they have to offer. It is not enough to design buildings: architects must open doors to what is possible and they have the techniques—the model, the perspective drawing, and the lecture—with which to do this. They have something to sell which is worth buying.

We are coming down to the level of architecture, to the built and (hopefully) the designed environment in which people live.

The first essential is that everything should be designed, the backs and sides as well as the fronts of buildings, the paving of streets as well as the skyline. The second desideratum is that everything should be designed well, and we have to accept the fact that there is not enough supreme genius about to allow the backs of warehouses being comparable with the works of Michelangelo or Mies van der Rohe. Designers can only do their best, but there is an obligation upon everyone who calls himself an architect to ensure that in every part of a building he has designed, whether it will be publicised or not, he *has* done his best as a designer. The Renaissance legacy of designing the front façade and leaving the back and sides to take care of themselves is not good enough. It never was very good and it derived from a silly theory (Alberti) that buildings need not be designed to be seen in perspective. (Alberti knew about perspective but did not apply it to architecture.)

Three problems emerge: the problem of humane aedicular architecture, the problem of socially significant architecture and the problem of beautiful architecture.

The problem of the architect who wants to express *himself* in architecture is of no interest to anybody else and is a proper study for psychotherapists.

Aedicular architecture is small in scale. Its maximal unit is the family dwelling. Detail design which can be appreciated at not more than ten metres distance determines its character. In terms of townscape it is expressed as a multiplicity, not as a unity. Decoration, individuation, variation in material and texture are to be used to give distinct individuality and yet preserve harmony between the components of a precinct. The basic social concept is the village, either in isolation or in an urban context. The successful town is a combination of villages around an urban nucleus. A village must be organic, that is capable of growth generated within it. It must have continuing design autonomy.

A domestic community has to have communal buildings. It is a nice sense of judgement, conditioned by the fashion of the time, which decides at what point aedicular architecture gives way to trilithonic. For example, a school may be idealised into a monumental building or domesticated so that it is an extension of the home, depending upon how one sees education, but the appropriateness of designing on one side or the other of the aedicular/trilithonic divide merits very serious consideration by the architect and the community for which he is working. How do they see their school? The architect should ask the question, not provide

the answer. In between is the old-fashioned functional answer—
a school is a place for teaching children. The result of this attitude
is a typical cubic assemblage.

All building exploits land and results in drastic ecological
changes. Domestic architecture is not only designed for man:
it is, or should be, designed for man in his environment. One may
seriously consider the value of overhanging eaves because of
house-martins. Much of man's enjoyment, more and more as
he gets older, comes from awareness of nature.

Architecture, as Ruskin said, has social significance but his
assessment of this (quoted on page 88), is very different from our
current ideas of social importance. We concentrate upon practical
welfare; he was aware of the significance of architecture as social
symbolism, providing not mundane amenities but embodiments
of ideals and aspirations. This is as much a part of social health
as a good drainage system.

The ideal of aedicular architecture is "the comfort and convenience of the inhabitants" combined with a non-predatory
relationship with the natural environment and a degree of symbolism appropriate to the character of the community. The
starting point is man and wife, what they need for their comfort,
their physical well-being, the growth of their family and its
education. As an individual, man needs a home, and this is the
basic stuff of architecture. As a member of a civilised community man needs architecture which symbolises whatever
principles, ideals and aspirations he may live by. This is public
architecture: it may tend towards the spiritual as in the medieval
parish church or towards the educational as in the twentieth-
century school or towards conviviality as in the English village
pub, or towards class-exclusiveness as in the working men's
club. In the big city, regional significances are important and the
need exists for people to feel that this is a different kind of place.
People don't want a city to be like a village or a housing estate.
The capital city has even more significance and people want
monumentality. But this book is not about monumental architecture, it is about humane architecture, architecture for people
and this is where the best design talents are needed.

The title of this chapter was A Theoretical Basis. What does it
amount to? Nothing elaborate; simply an insistence that architecture should be for the enjoyment of people, not perfect people
for these will never be, but man in all his variety and imperfection.
The measure of architecture and of planning is not some idealistic
conception of man but men and women and children as they

really are. The architect's job is to design for them with sympathy and empathy. It is none of his business to reform mankind but if architects give of their best they can contribute a lot to improving the human condition. It is their duty to let people know what they can give, and, having promised, to perform.

# chapter 14
# Practical Application

It is not the purpose of this book, indeed it would be presumptuous, to try to tell architects how to design. We have been concerned with the basic theory of architecture, why architecture exists, why it matters, what architects can do for mankind and what people need from architects. To leave it at this, without considering, if only briefly, what practical action should follow if the argument which we have considered is judged to be valid, would be an evasion of a commitment which, I think, every writer of a theoretical book should accept; namely, to consider the practical implications of his theories.

It has been suggested that the modern movement was no more than a transition towards an architecture which, we hope, will be far better and more interesting than anything the twentieth century has yet produced. Probably it is useless to preach to seasoned practitioners, most of whom are set in their ways, so the suggestions that follow are directed to students and younger architects and all who are concerned with architectural education on the one hand and to those who commission architecture, the architects' patrons, on the other.

Architects can only do what their patrons allow them to do and it is of the utmost importance that architects should speak clearly to the public about architecture and what it can do and mean to them. The main prejudice which has to be overcome rests upon hidden political, social and economic ideas and beliefs which stand in the way of the creation of a much better environment for living people. We have already noticed that the three-cornered conflict of architects, contractors and workers makes it almost impossible to achieve really good environmental conditions. Apart from saying so, architects are almost powerless to alter this situation; but they must state loudly and clearly that the present organisation of the building industry is outrageously unsatisfactory. It is not enough to blame management; even more important is the attitude of labour which, by many of its habitual practices, is defeating the aims of most socially concerned people to provide a decent environment for everybody. The trade unions have a not ignoble record of striving to better the conditions of their members and possibly thereby to raise standards generally, though this consequence is becoming less and less credible nowadays. Unfortunately, amelioration almost always has been seen in terms of increased wages, but what really matters in a society is not the amount of money people have but the conditions in which they live. So I would plead, and I hope all architects will support this plea, for a realignment of trade union thinking so that environmental conditions are given higher priority than mere wages. The effect of concentrating simply upon economic means of betterment is unfortunately contributing to the deterioration of our environment. The trades unions concerned with building have a particular responsibility in this matter: if they are sincere in their social concern they must realise that the quality of the environment for all people depends upon *their* work to a very large extent.

The control of land-use has been discussed in Chapters 7 and 8. This control should be directed towards the conservation of resources and the use of land in such ways as will contribute most effectively to the quality of the environment in which we live. At present we are besottedly obsessed with road transport and the provision of a great many buildings, such as prestige office blocks, which are of very doubtful social value. Furthermore, our structural methods, involving the massive use of concrete, create buildings which will be extremely difficult to demolish. Whereas old types of structure could generally be demolished and removed so that land could be restored to something like its previous usage, modern building is making permanent wounds on the face of the earth. Serious consideration should be given to legislation making it compulsory for buildings to be constructed in such a way that they can be removed without leaving permanent scars. This at least would ensure that mistakes can be rectified. At present we are making a great many mistakes which will be there for ever.

We have seen that land values are created by "permitted use" and if we are to have sensible planning, land values must be eliminated from the problem. Land should be used in the best possible way and not misused because it has acquired some artificially created value. In a civilised society all land-use and building should be directed towards the creation of a better environment, towards a better way of life.

The idea that a building should be erected as cheaply as possible is merely another way of saying that we do not care about architecture. Good quality is not cheap and if we are to have modern architecture which we can enjoy as much as most people enjoy the best architecture of earlier times, we must be prepared to pay for it. This does not mean that we can simply get good architecture by making our buildings expensive. It does mean that we cannot have really good architecture on the cheap. Further-more, the costs of the various components in buildings need to be studied more carefully than they have been: in much modern building there are great extravagances, particularly on the engin-eering and services side and sometimes in the choice of design-forms by architects, of which the general public and, indeed, the actual clients for the buildings are not aware. Sculpture, for example, may seem to be an obvious extravagance because its cost is isolated in the bill. But the choice of a lavish heating system, or form of structure, or window type may go completely unnoticed. People who pay for buildings should be aware of what they are paying for. Much apparently cheap architecture is, in fact, very dear. And, there is the question of maintenance: many buildings which are cheap to build are extremely costly to maintain. Also, many advocates of standardisation and mechanisation in architecture fail to observe that the main-tenance of these "rationalised" and mechanised buildings can only be done by hand-work. It is absolute nonsense to construct so-called rationalised buildings in which handcraft is reduced to a minimum when their maintenance is going to depend quite excessively upon tedious, and in the case of high buildings, often very dangerous hand-work.

Turning to architects themselves and schools of architecture in which, above all, one would hope to see signs of a new concern for creating architecture which is pleasant for people and con-tributory to a physically and spiritually healthy environment, there are a number of fields of study which need to be cultivated.

Firstly, the architectural profession needs to use every possible means to build up its awareness of the actual needs of people. We need a new subject—architectural psychology—which is concerned with people's feelings in relation to their environment, the bases of their evaluation, the importance of symbolism, meaning, home, relationships and continuity, their response to textures and colours, the effects of massing, the problems of scale relationships, the sense of place, recognition symbols, family patterns, geriatric problems, the right size of buildings, the value of diversity and of employing different designers for adjacent buildings, the effects of thinking too big, of monotony, and the imposition of so-called design values upon people whether they like them or not, the architectural causes of vandalism and delinquency. The list could be extended almost indefinitely and it is a sad fact that, though a certain amount of lip-service is paid to social concern in schools of architecture, there is, in fact, very little awareness of, care for, or systematised knowledge about what people *really* need. Far too often, architects are simply big brother knowing what he wants to give people and determined to make them like it.

Secondly architects need to give a great deal of consideration to the nature of their work, the nature of their responsibilities to society, and they need to revise their concept of professional good conduct so as to give priority to good architecture and environmental design. Perhaps the major stumbling block is that architects do not think of people as individuals and families; they think of groups, classes, types, not of actual human beings. Among the major diseases of modern society is anomy, a sense which people have of *not mattering*. Architects, in common with members of other professions, most of industrial management, and practically all bureaucrats, contribute to the spread of this disease which leads to neuroses, crime, and vandalism and is antithetical to the very idea of civilisation.

Thirdly, the basic theory of architecture needs to be studied afresh and I would suggest that the best way of beginning this is by the comparative study of known theories of architecture—absolute theories, subjective, sociological, functional, associative, elemental, etc.—and anti-theories, such as mannerism, anarchism, and expressionism. The advantage of such a study would be to open architects' minds to the enormous range of architectural possibilities which are at present neglected and perhaps, by encouraging philosophical thought about architecture, to lead to the generation of new concepts.

Fourthly, we should be aware of the determinants of architectural change, social, political, economic and ideological. This does not mean that architects should study sociology, politics, etc. except in so far as these subjects impinge upon the actual practice of architecture, but it does mean that they should think about conditions in which they work and the limitations which are imposed upon them in a practical and creative way.

Fifthly, the nature of architectural experience needs to be studied; this follows from architectural philosophy and architectural psychology. Perception theory, perspective and theories of space, such as those developed by Le Corbusier,[1] need to be studied as a way of developing disciplined architectural thought.

Sixthly, we need to consider relationships and, in particular, the limits of architecture; where does it begin and end, what are its relationships with other activities? It is merely silly to talk of the "total" involvement of the architect in "total architecture". The architect has to define his rôle and it follows from this that we should study the nature of the profession, its functions, whether it needs to contain people who are not architects— such as historians, scientists, economists who have specialised in architecture—and the meaning of professional standards.

Seventhly, though we have already mentioned significance and symbolism under previous headings, these need to be studied in specific contexts and we need to look at such problems as dignity, popularity, vulgarity, fun, awe, reverence, and so on.

Eighthly, there is the question of the relationship of architecture with the other arts. It has almost always been assumed in the past that there was a relationship and that many of the other arts should find their most important opportunities within the context of building. Architects have gone off on their own and become lost in a desert. The bringing-together of the arts is a necessity for good architecture, but this means adjustments and some drastic changes in the teaching and practice of such arts as painting and sculpture.

Finally, belief in architecture is only one aspect of *belief*. To enjoy good architecture, a society must have beliefs, it must have faith in a way of life. The worship of money is getting us nowhere: it is indeed destroying the world.

# Postscript
# Art and the Architect

I have divided architecture into two kinds. One is the aedicular which is for people to live and work in. Most building is of this kind and all of it should be architecture; it should be congenial, comfortable, as pleasing to the senses as possible. The other kind is symbolic. It has no necessary function other than to be symbolic, to mean something to people, to stand as architecture for something greater than themselves, more enduring.

But in art there are three kinds. The first, as in architecture, is for people, to serve their daily needs whether they be physical or emotional. Then there is the artistic equivalent of monumental architecture, art which is communal, larger than man and more enduring. But the third kind has no architectural equivalent because it is purely for the person who makes it. Art can be, and I think should be, a means of exploration and understanding of oneself and one's environment for everybody and it should be part of a good education to cultivate the practice of art for personal experience. Such art is not for sale or fame. It is something everyone should do, not least the architect who, because as an artist he cultivates his sensitivity, has a special need to practise art for himself. I shall not elaborate this theme here because it is the subject of another book, but if we think of art in these three categories, *vernacular* or folk art is generally comfortable and beloved. *Great art*, as we evaluate it, was nearly always done for an ulterior motive, whether it was at the level of early English water colours done for engravers of topographical books, altar pieces in Baroque churches, symphonies for concert performance, or the ceiling of the Sistine Chapel. Great art seems to require of the artist that he works for a non-artistic purpose and yet can use that purpose as a vehicle. *Personal art* is part of a full life and may be anything the artist wishes it to be. Only by chance will it have any value to anyone else.

Because of the nature of architecture there are times when an architect, though a sensitive artist, cannot find personal fulfilment and tends to be frustrated by the conditions of architectural

99

practice. I would advocate that every architect should engage in some other art form, as Le Corbusier practised painting. It is thus possible to keep separate one's private and one's public rôle as an artist. The purity of Le Corbusier's architecture probably owed much to the fact that he was also a painter. If the architect is truly to produce architecture for people he must always put them first in his professional work and it is much easier for him to do this if he practises another art in a personal way.

# Notes

CHAPTER 1

1. For architects there is an intellectual component in aesthetics. This was best expressed by the neo-platonists and Thomas Aquinas. Perhaps the most emotionally evocative architecture was the medieval cathedrals, yet these were intellectually conceived.
2. *Sympathy* is "feeling-with" and this is the starting point for an intellectual process of ministering to that which has been apprehended by sympathy. *Empathy* is deliberate sympathy: it is the act of feeling oneself into.
3. "The hog of multitude", William Wilbur, *Poems 1943–1956* (London, 1957).
4. Le Corbusier, *Vers une Architecture* (Paris, 1923).

CHAPTER 2

1. This is an excessively simplistic view. Gropius himself believed in the value of craftsmanship and the great schism in the Bauhaus was partly a result of the *failure* to reconcile hand-craftsmanship and design for machine-production.
2. The idea that there is an inherent morphology of materials has ceased to be convincing. Modern materials can be moulded to an almost infinite variety of forms. Form is not inherent in material; certainly not in modern materials such as steel and plastics.
3. I myself subscribed to this view in *A General History of Architecture* (London, 1955). One of the best modern refutations is in *House Form and Culture* by Amos Rapoport (Englewood Cliffs, N.J., 1969).
4. Michelangelo, *Sonnet*.
5. The classical ideal perhaps best expressed by Alberti in *De Re Aedificatoria* (1485). "Beauty, modesty, gracefulness and the like charms consist in those particulars which, if you alter or take away, the whole would be made homely and disagreeable".
6. Specific art is allusive but not necessarily representational. Representation is always and inevitably specific.
7. There is an element of specificity in all these, especially Klee and Miro.
8. The basic art course is a curious amalgam of Itten's *Vorkurs* at the Bauhaus which was supposed to be based upon understanding the nature of materials and, at the other extreme, the Pasmore-Hamilton fusion of modernistic pastiche and dadaism. It seems to be on its way out.
9. The idea that a student should be purged of all previous prejudice and experience is, it seems to me, a psychologically dangerous procedure. At its best it conditions the student to stylistic modernism. At its worst it destroys him.
10. As Professor Banham has pointed out, in *Theory and Design in the First Machine Age* (London, 1960), most of the Bauhaus teachers were expressionists. It is ironical that German expressionism has been transmitted to art education through the Bauhaus when Gropius himself was essentially intellectual rather than expressionist.

11. *L'Architecture* (Paris, 1567).
12. Functionalism: I have discussed this in *Art and the Nature of Architecture* (London, 1952).
13. Why then call it functionalism? Functionalism, as generally understood, leaves out the human component in the problem or, not infrequently, misunderstands it as, for example, in the design of aircraft seats which only permit the occupant one position.
14. Ironically the word manufacture, which originally meant *hand-making*, has become corrupted since the industrial revolution to mean *machine-making* of goods.
15. I have discussed this at length in *Civilization, the Next Stage* (Newcastle upon Tyne, 1969).

CHAPTER 3

1. Inigo Jones (Sketch book, 1614).
2. A good example is Boullée in the French revolution period.
3. The treason of the artists is the desertion of their artistic commitment to civilisation.
4. Alberti and Le Corbusier were both architects who wrote about the philosophy of architecture. Alberti clearly used his buildings to exemplify his theories and profoundly distrusted his innate artistic ability. Le Corbusier, on the other hand, seems to have used writing to explain and justify his architecture.
5. This is not a plea for élitism which, indeed, has nothing to do with real quality. See below p. 33 sqq.
6. See p. 18 above.
7. This is a curious paradox, that a system supposedly devoted to enterprise avoids risk as far as possible by voluntary collectivisation of risk to the enrichment of insurance companies. But it is the side-effect that really matters, the availability to financiers of enormous funds for manipulation.

CHAPTER 4

1. Banham, P. R., *Theory and Design in the First Machine Age* (p. 329) (London, 1960).
2. In the U.S.A., which had escaped devastation and emerged rich from the war, there was some swing away towards the romanticism of F. L. Wright. Post-war American architecture is too big and complex a subject to discuss in this context but, briefly, architectural thinking seems to have been escapist.
3. Exemplified in his curious Reith Lectures on *The Englishness of English Art* (BBC, 1956).
4. London, 1936.
5. Most of the Bauhaus artists were reared in Expressionism.
6. See Banham, P. R., *op. cit.*
7. The history of architecture suggests that architects have nearly always been slow to adjust to new social conditions. The reason is partly that they depend upon people who have money and these are usually old and often reactionary people; but there is also the sad fact, as it can be seen at present, that architects do not read enough and fail to keep up with ideas outside their profession, partly because architecture is so fascinating a subject, but it is a dangerous neglect.
8. In *Chamber's Encyclopaedia*.
9. Architectural Press, 1959.
10. As is emphasised later, art is not primarily concerned with self-expression nor is it antithetical to science.

### Chapter 5

1. See Young, M., *The Rise of the Meritocracy* (London, 1958). (IQ + effort = MERIT.)
2. Actually "All animals are equal but some animals are more equal than others". Orwell, G., *Animal Farm* (London, 1945).
3. See also Allsopp, B., *Civilization, the Next Stage* (Newcastle, 1969).

### Chapter 6

1. Bye-law housing is a British term applied mainly to housing resulting from Bye-law control after the 1875 Public Health Act.
2. The phrase is from Paolo Soleri: "There is no way of simulating the interaction of non-rational entities", i.e. human people (*The Guardian*, 14.11.72).
3. It has to be recognised that political and business interests often operate together both on the left and the right.

### Chapter 7

1. This is just as true on the political left as on the right. People who have privilege or power tend to approve the source of that privilege or power.
2. The prestige office block may well be compared with the Renaissance palace, the triumph of ostentation over common sense and the prelude to collapse.
3. *Civilization, the Next Stage, op. cit.*
4. Cf. ch. 4, p. 28.
5. It is outrageous to educate people, as we do, and then deny them the environmental facilities to be what they have been educated to be. As things are education can be an incentive to crime.
6. Modern planners put business interests first and environmental quality very low down the list of priorities. It is more important that we should be able to live in a satisfactory environment than that the grocer should be able to deliver his goods at the minimum inconvenience and cost to himself.
7. The present practice of sending costly executive personnel by air from place to place is becoming an economic anachronism. The tradition of business hospitality could be maintained by reversing the charges!

### Chapter 8

1. This is the horrible fact. Until education of our bureaucrats has gone far above present levels a major obstruction to good environmental design will be the low quality of administrators.
2. It is silly to question the sincerity of a rich socialist and not to question the sincerity of a poor socialist.

### Chapter 9

1. James Stirling speaking at a students' symposium in Newcastle, February 1973.
2. Le Corbusier, *Vers une Architecture* (Paris, 1923).
3. To be aware he must be well informed and critical. All too often architects seem to be dazzled by mountebanks.
4. Bath was developed by John Wood, father and son, in the eighteenth century.

## Chapter 10

1. Laugier, M-A, *Observations sur l'Architecture* (Paris, 1765).
2. Summerson, J., *Heavenly Mansions* (London, 1949). *Aedicula* is the diminutive of *aedes*, Latin for "a building for habitation".
3. In painting it is difficult to make architecture subordinate. It tends to dominate the picture, virtually to become the subject matter of the picture.
4. *Concise Oxford Dictionary*.
5. In *The Landscape of Ideas* (London, 1972).
6. Sir Titus Salt built an "ideal" industrial town called Saltaire on the river Aire in Yorkshire, England. 1850 to 1863.
7. It was a perverse act of masochism when British Rail demolished it.
8. Castle Howard, Yorkshire, England, designed by Sir John Vanbrugh.
9. Blenheim House, nr. Oxford, England, also by Vanbrugh.

## Chapter 11

1. In *Education and Self-Expression* (in preparation at the time of writing).
2. Cf. *The Sparkling Stone* by Jan van Ruysbroeck, ". . . in an eternal death to ourselves".
3. Here I use the word *eclecticism* in its normal critical sense as an attitude to design whereby stylistic features are selected from the past. There is a new sense, or rather a reshaping of the old philosophical meaning of eclecticism, which sees it as a next and necessary stage in the evolution of civilisation. This is expounded by Jon Wynne-Tyson in *The Civilised Alternative* (Fontwell and London, 1972).
4. A distinction must be made between genuine folk art and modern pop art which is based upon cynical, totally non-artistic commercialism.

## Chapter 12

1. The inflexible design and administration of housing estates often makes the development of a healthily creative community impossible.

## Chapter 13

1. I have suggested earlier (ch. 10) that communities (if that word is appropriate) which are selfish, disrespectful and lacking in faith cannot have a valid monumental architecture. By faith I do not mean religious faith in the ordinary Christian sense but *belief outside of self*. Where such belief exists I suspect that the distinction between old and modern becomes irrelevant and much of the self-conscious posturing of self-conscious "modernists" looks ridiculous.
2. I have developed this idea in *Ecological Morality* (London, 1972, published in New York with the title *The Garden Earth*).
3. They may also be spiritual and this may be emotional, intellectual or something else.
4. Ruskin, J., *Seven Lamps of Architecture*, 1849.
5. Tolstoy, L., *What is Art?* (ch. X).
"A good and lofty work of art may be incomprehensible, but not to simple, unperverted peasant labourers (all that is highest is understood by them)— it may be, and often is, unintelligible to erudite, perverted people . . .". Cf. "Only the people who live in the villages understand." Wump Wan of New Guinea (BBC, February 1973).
6. I certainly do *not* advocate this.

CHAPTER 14

1.  Dr. G. H. Baker has made a profound analysis of these in *Le Corbusier and the Articulation of Architectural Elements* (unpublished at time of going to press). Professor N. L. Prak in *The Language of Architecture* and more recently is a leader in this field.

# Index